YOUR NAME HERE !
HOW TO GET THE THEME PARK OR RESORT ROLE OF YOUR DREAMS

By

Ronald Fox

Boca Raton, Florida

www.ronfoxmedia.com

TABLE OF CONTENTS

INTRODUCTION
SO...YOU WANT TO WORK AT A THEME PARK
SO...YOU WORK AT A THEME PARK
SO...YOU WORKED AT A THEME PARK
SO...YOU WANT TO HIRE A FORMER THEME PARK EMPLOYEE
ADDITIONAL INSIGHTS
BIOGRAPHY
ACKNOWLEDGEMENTS

INTRODUCTION

When speaking with current and former theme park employees, my goal was simple: I wanted them to share their experiences, but I also wanted them to share what they wished they could have known before going in for that first interview, audition, or business transfer. The benefit is greatest when we have insight from those who have traveled down the path before us.

The focus of this book is simple: how to transform your desire to become part of a theme park operation - or your existing experience with the industry - into an actionable plan within or beyond the world of theme parks and resorts. This book is a window into my experiences at various theme parks, both in the U.S. and abroad, including Disney, Universal, and Six Flags. It is also a collection of carefully curated stories, drawn from hundreds of hours of conversation with current and former employees of theme parks, resorts, and cruise lines. Many of these chats were with peers, while others were with friendly faces who eagerly stepped forward to share their insights and, in some cases, their dos and don'ts for theme park work.

Although I was only with Disney for a few years longer than my tenure with Universal, my career path and growth there was more dynamic. Where Universal was linear, Disney was a spider-legged trajectory. There was overlap in some of my responsibilities, like content development partnership, training, and special events, but I traveled farther on the shoulders of giants while at the House of the Mouse. As a result, if this book feels a little more weighted towards Disney, you understand why. So devour this book for the stories, and thoughtfully chew and digest the insights you find within.

Many people have heard the expression, "That is a Mickey Mouse operation." Such a comment is something of an insult, deprecating and intended to point out how cheap or poorly thought out something is. This is the reality: anything and everything that found its genesis in association with Mickey Mouse is simultaneously multi-tiered and multi-faceted. The reach goes farther than you might think. This includes Disney's cast members, Universal team members, Six Flags team members, the Disney Cruise Line crew, and their training. With all the levels of complexity that go into everything from designing and building a theme park resort or restaurant, to launching a Disney Cruise, such dismissive comments are curious to consider.

When you visit a Universal theme park, think about how carefully your trip is being managed. Regardless of how you arrive at the resort or park, there are people there to influence and frame your state of mind. Team members (Universal employees) in merchandise can give you an idea on how to plan your day, people at the refreshment stand will advise you on which park to start with and which attractions to hit first, and the greeters will tell you which restaurants or quick serve locations have the best options for a range of diets and tastes. Everyone, regardless of the park or location, will engage you and your family, in most cases without you having to initiate the conversation. That's a keystone to excellent customer service and it is taught from the first day on the job. Don't let anyone tell you the personal touch is lost in big companies. Even with the advances in technology and AI current and still to come, nothing in the world in which we live can replace the authentic vibration of human interaction. The reality is that with the right expectations, boundaries, and introduction to company culture, you can create a legion of ambassadors for your brand. In the entertainment theme park arena, Disney and Universal both accomplish this because brand new employees learn how important they are to the brand itself from day one. Sure, they're being hired into a job to perform a task, but that is only one part of the equation. People will gladly spend money and frequently patronize an establishment where the food is better than okay, but the service is out of this world. Conversely, one can dine at a five-star resort restaurant where the food is prepared by a Michelin chef, but the service is terrible; that place will go out of business. It's the connection and the relationships that people want, even if they don't realize this in the moment. At most places where a brisk business is accomplished, you'll see the staff wearing more than one hat of responsibility. Your seater may also run food, or your manager maybe bussing tables.

A mistake that is unintentionally but frequently made when it comes to any major theme park operation is understanding what a particular role entails. Entertainment companies like Disney and Universal provide training directives with such precision that it's easy to take for granted the simplicity of the process as it is displayed in guest-facing locations. That is not by accident. But unlike just about any other business or industry in the world, what you do in your theme park position is never as straightforward as the initial role or job title suggests.

When I worked overseas, I never once heard my friend Leon say, "That's not my job." What he would say instead was, *"Waarom niet,"* which means *why not.* That particular year, he was the lighting designer and tech for our stage, but he could often be found working alongside maintenance for one of the park rides, or any number of other things not in his job description. For Ton, another Dutch friend, he'd just as easily be found in guest relations, translating, as he would performing on our stage as host. View your job title as a starting point and the first step.

For example, if you work in a quick-serve food and beverage location, you are not just responsible for serving food. You're tracking inventory in real time, managing guest expectations, and keeping up with the latest training as required by federal, state, and company guidelines. You are also empowered to engage in guest service recovery: if you see somebody walking away from your counter with an order of french fries that then falls to the floor, you don't have to call the manager or fill out a form. You don't have to send them to guest relations or go through any process to refund the loss. You simply smile at the guest and hand them a new basket of fries - not because this is the solution that grabbed you at the time, but because you've been trained for things like this, even if you wouldn't find this experience described anywhere in the title of Food and Beverage, Quick Serve.

When you're a manager at any operation in a theme park, you are essentially the captain and the operation is your ship. In addition to being responsible for everything mentioned previously, you're also managing daily staffing, budgeting, and maintenance issues, all the while serving as an ambassador for your department and the greater complex itself. You have to deal with resident communication platforms, plug-ins that do everything from squawk challenges at you to identifying projected inventory and staffing needs. In any forward-leaning operation, a person wearing a name tag that says "Manager" doesn't only manage, they *also* manage.

When you find yourself looking at a résumé with Disney, Universal, SeaWorld, Six Flags, or any other theme park or resort name on it, this should be treated as an invitation to query. No matter what title appears on a former theme park employee's CV, the true extent to what they bring to the table as an applicant can be discovered by asking questions and peeling back the layers of the time they spent with their company. This applicant is worth a second look. Theme parks are single-handedly responsible for producing more executives who started out working in unskilled labor (busboys, greeters, performers, etc.) than is possible to count. Such a trajectory is designed into these company operations: begin at day one with orientation and develop over time into tomorrow's leaders. Such tracking is not dictatorial. Plenty of people go to work at parks and resorts, happy to remain in their position, in a specific line of business, for years and decades.

If you have left the magical world of theme park employment and are trying to figure out what the next chapter of your work-life looks like, be prepared to describe above and beyond your job title. An entertainment company name is a neon sign on a CV. This includes destination resorts and cruise lines. Look for opportunities to talk about your time there, and trust that the hiring manager in front of you is eager to engage with you regarding your experience.

There are a metric ton of how-to books out there, applicable to every conceivable industry. The topics of these books range from how to get a raise to how to land the job of your dreams. My motivation for writing this book is a little different. I want to form a connection. My conversations with other theme park employees, current and former, became the catalyst for this project. In sales, there is an expression: facts tell and stories sell. I believe that excellent storytelling sells itself by locking down the emotions and creating a connection. I have decades of comprehensive experience working in parks. I've been an attractions host and leader at Disney, a stuntman and trainer with Universal, an orientation facilitator and trainer with the Disney Cruise Line, and both a bartender and entertainer with Six Flags (but not at the same time). As you read on, you'll discover that is just the start. Being a connector means I learn a great deal from others and look for ways to share those learnings. With this background, I knew that I could bring story after story to the table. Through the stories of my own and others, I get to connect with you, the reader. Offering insight on how to best apply yourself to finding opportunities inside and beyond the theme park and resort industry is just one part. We humans are not solitary creatures. Even when we are independent contributors, we are part of a pod. Whenever I hear someone say, "There is no *'I'* in team, but there is a *'me'*," I like to tell them, "That's correct, and *you* are part of a team." The word 'team', by its definition, means collective. When we all work together, we get more accomplished. I am here to help you accomplish whatever your goals and dreams are. My recommendation? Read the entire book.

If you've left the theme park world, reading the section on what to do after you've left, or the section on how to hire a Disney cast member will clue you in on tips for pursuing the next steps of your career. If your time in attractions operations is so far in your rearview mirror that it almost feels like a dream, it's still worth revisiting. Even if you're not planning on returning to a life working at a theme park or resort, that experience can inform and impress upon your present day almost as much as your childhood experiences. It is no different than the life lessons we learned as children and carry into adulthood. If you're a hiring manager and you see a theme park company or entertainment operation on a résumé, reading the sections on working at a theme park can give you a better idea of what it really means to have been a Disney cast member or a Universal team member, and it can help you better understand the sense of community and relationship-building that goes into working at such an operation.

Some points will be revisited in all sections of this book - I believe that these are the stand-out elements of theme park work most informative to the whole experience. Other points might be unique to a particular company, and the attention paid to them will be appropriately narrow in scope.

This is not an officially sanctioned or authorized book. I did not seek permission or direction from Disney, Universal, Six Flags, or any other entertainment company to write this book. My desire is to share perspective and warmth through the insight, stories, trivia and facts I've gathered from my time in this industry. The stories and insights I share, are all relevant to the various sections in this book. If I had shared every personal story and experience, the important details and message might've gotten lost. For example, the shenanigans and practical jokes really do not have a place here, but it doesn't make them any less entertaining to tell. On the other hand, the stories here provide additional perspective on how to find the right doors and open those doors to opportunity. Speaking of opportunity, The section titles reference theme parks, but the information here is just as applicable to the resort, cruise line and broader entertainment industry. The ideas and lessons here apply just about anywhere.

I wrote the book I wish existed when I first fell in love with the world of the theme park years ago. I wrote this book to share the humanity behind the experience. Mine was not a perfect experience, but it was my experience, and a great one, nonetheless. In regards to both Universal and Disney, where countless people I know got hired or cast after their first audition, I interviewed with both organizations over and over and over again, only to be met with the all-too-familiar, "Thank you" acknowledging that I was free to go.

It was Lee, a friend's mom and ever-present entity in my life, whose encouragement kept me from giving up. In some ways, this book is a tremendous note of gratitude to her for telling me, "This could be the time." This wasn't something she repeated over and over again. She said it once, at the right time. She was right and I was headed for the Disney/MGM soundstages. More auditions later I was hired for Universal's "The Wild Wild Wild West Stunt Show". Multiple auditions for Universal later, this would prove the first of many live shows I'd perform in.

If it's Disney, Universal, or another theme park or entertainment venue role you're after, then the thing I also want you to take away from this book is to *never, ever give up*. Dreams do come true. That's not just me trying to sprinkle pixie dust far and wide. There are too many examples out there to ignore, too many people who pressed forward and realized their dreams.

I am one of them.

I welcome your thoughts and insights, and hope you enjoy the book. Please feel free to reach out to me at <u>www.ronfoxmedia.com</u>. Hit the contact button to send me a note.

Wishing you magic on your journey,
Ron

PREFACE

D isney and Universal do a more thorough job of researching the individual applying for a position than just about any other company in any other industry, anywhere in the world. Whether it's for security, food and beverage, or backstage support, they are very particular about who they hire - with evaluations on the front end and background checks on the back end of the hiring process. If you're going to work on the Disney Cruise Line, additional background checks enter the picture. They are thorough. This doesn't mean that if you stumbled in judgement somewhere in your past, it will be an insurmountable obstacle to teaching a Muggle how to wave their wand just so, with a swish and flick. These companies recognize everyone deserves a second chance to fly. Just remember to be forthright on your application.

Regardless the theme park, getting hired is a big deal. These companies invest time and money into training new employees. Day One of both Disney and Universal orientation was one of the most magical days of my theme park career. It is no ordinary onboarding, "Here are your documents, sign them, do your computer compliance, and welcome aboard," handshake experience. Universal and Disney make it special, investing tens of thousands of dollars into the training process. Whether someone is going into accounting, becoming an admin assistant, an Actors' Equity covered show, working food and beverage or attractions operations, every single individual who goes through orientation walks away with the same foundational knowledge as their peers, as well as the understanding that working in a theme park is more than a job. A tremendous amount of value is seen in the individual receiving their very first Disney or Universal name tag. Getting your first name tag in orientation is celebrated, literally and figuratively. From the very beginning, you are introduced to and immersed in a culture that clearly delineates expectations.

Whether you are looking to become a Disney cast member, a Universal team member, part of a cruise line crew, part of another team, or you want to maximize the potential of your experience, know that these companies have invested a tremendous amount of energy in your success. A job at a theme park is more than a landing platform, it is a launchpad with stratospheric capacity and capability. Whether you stay and grow with the entertainment organization you join, or grow beyond, this is where the next step of that career starts. Every single individual at every one of these parks and resorts started with the same thing you have: drive, dreams, and desire.

SO...YOU WANT TO WORK AT A THEME PARK

For many people, the Disney siren song is strong. For others, it is the call to the Muggle, encouraging them to reach for the wizard within. Some remember that western show they saw as a kid and have to be part of that magic. Others fell in love with the idea of making a different animal out of towels every night. Some want to work with animals, others respond to the call of the sea. It was Disney for me. The first time I went to the Walt Disney World Resort, I was with friends. We rode the ferry boat over, seeing the spires of Cinderella Castle beckoning in the distance. When we stepped onto the landing to disembark, a train whistled as it pulled away from Main Street Station, just as the monorail passed overhead. No movie intro could have done better. Except for the Texas State Fair, I'd never seen so many people in one place moving as a collective, amorphic swarm anywhere else in the world. People seemed to be coming from everywhere, all heading more or less towards the park entrance, a merging, living braided conveyor belt of humanity. We got through the turnstiles with our tickets and walked through the tunnel beneath the station. Even that was an assault on the senses. The smell of popcorn and excitement, the music and the smiles of the crowd surging around us was exhilarating. Emerging from the tunnel and walking up to the base of Main Street, there at the end of Main Street USA was the prettiest thing I had ever seen: Cinderella's castle.

Later I would learn that every element down to the smallest detail of the entrance design was intentional, just as it was at every other Disney park. I would also discover, decades later, that the train station is the show curtain for the Magic Kingdom itself. But walking up Main Street for the first time, I knew none of this. That day, I must have been moving slower than the rest of my friends because the next time I looked over to comment on the smell of fudge, I found myself talking to a stranger. I looked to my other side and saw a couple of cast members waving with big, gloved Mickey hands. They made it look like so much fun, and they were getting paid! At that moment I knew I had to be a part of this place, to make this kind of magic. Sign. Me. Up. I was determined to work for Disney, to become a cast member. I didn't know how it would happen, only that it would.

That was my moment. When was yours? Maybe it hasn't happened yet.

During my inaugural day as a Disney guest, we probably rode the Haunted Mansion close to a dozen times. Every trip we took back to the ride of 999 happy haunts, there were fewer of us. The last couple of times, I was riding alone. To this day, there's something about that attraction that captivates me. And if I rode the Haunted Mansion a dozen times, I rode Pirates of the Caribbean at least half as many. After my first ride on Space Mountain, we walked through the exit, and I immediately turned around and headed right back in. I was met by a smiling, redheaded cast member named Theresa, who said jokingly, "Where do you think you're going?"

I smiled at her dumbly, not really having an answer. Even though I was obviously going back in line, I didn't know if my reason was just to ride again. I was still overwhelmed by the experience, and my brain was going off the rails processing everything my eyes were seeing. I asked her if she liked working for Disney, and she told me she enjoyed it greatly. She told me her dad was part of the opening team and was an executive, working as part of the project team to open a then brand-new park called Epcot Center.

Theresa offered to be my tour guide the next time I came to Disney, and we exchanged contact information. She reached out to me about a month and a half later to tell me that Epcot Center was doing a cast member friends-and-family tour. She wanted to know if I was interested. You bet I was.

I drove up the day before the tour and stayed with Theresa and her family. They lived in Winter Haven, a town I would grow to love for its history, and the friends I would make. The next day, Theresa, several of her friends, and I went down to the park. The tour was conducted in one of the parking lot trams, starting where the actual parking lot would be built and extending up the path to where the World Showcase Lagoon now sits. Everywhere you looked was all hard-hat areas, massive earthmovers, and piles of dirt several stories tall. Spaceship Earth stood as a spherical skeletal structure with a veiny track partially assembled inside. Big metal plates marked where vehicles would go. The tour took us right into the middle of the hustle and bustle. It was the construction equivalent of a downtown metropolitan area during pedestrian rush hour. So many people. I had never been so excited about something, not since I stepped foot into the Magic Kingdom for the first time.

After the tour we went out as a group to eat, and I peppered everyone with questions. Almost everybody there worked in attractions operations, but a few of the cast members were entertainment technicians or Kids of the Kingdom dancers (KoKs they call themselves, and we could have made a drinking game out of the number of times they referred to themselves by that acronym). I asked how people got their jobs there. The answers I received varied, but the one similarity (apart from the dancers, who were recruited through auditions) was that they lived in central Florida when they applied. I was told Disney gave preference to people who lived in the area.

The residency requirement is not really a thing anymore. Depending on the role you're hired for, they will give you a relocation allowance or stipend. When I went to apply, I got a place at the Saint Cloud Motel to have a local address. I showed up to the trailer behind the Magic Kingdom, which served as the casting/hiring facility for the entire property. For my interview I was sporting my brand-new dress shirt. About five minutes into the interview, the person on the other side of the table told me that Disney appreciated my interest, but I wasn't exactly what they were looking for. He did encourage me to apply again in the future. As you can no doubt guess, this wouldn't be the last time I stepped foot into a casting building. I was disappointed, to say the least. After several similarly fruitless auditions (over the course of many years), I ended up getting hired and cast for "The Wild Wild Wild West Stunt Show" at Universal. That audition taught me a little more about the laid-back yet professional nature of the entertainment division at Universal.

For example, when I was in the room for the Universal audition, the first thing they asked was if I had ever fallen off a horse. I wasn't trying to be funny when I said, "Yes, but not on purpose." That got a laugh and possibly may have been the reason for the call back. I followed with my monologue, and they asked me to stick around. When I went in for a call-back, the casting team wanted to know about my stunt background and my experiences with horses. I was forthright and told them I had grown up in rural Texas, so I had been around horses since I was old enough to walk. It didn't make me a horse whisperer, but it was good enough that they invited me to come in for the practical, riding portion of the audition.

The first time I went to Universal as a guest, I had press credentials from the University I attended. We went for the grand opening, a gala-event style grand unveiling of the park. The park itself had been a resounding nightmare. A terrible storm had come through the day prior and incapacitated several of the attractions by frying computers, and even some of the features within each attraction. Crowds were unmanageable, and celebrities were heading for the exits. It was not the park's best moment. Years later and a few months after I was hired, I slowly began to see what magic existed beyond the walls of Walt Disney World. At Universal, I would go to Café La Bamba for lunch then head to Finnegan's after my shows wrapped for the day, where I came across guests and other team members who recognized me and struck up conversations. It reminded me a bit of the stories. My grandmother would tell me when she worked at Columbia pictures. Back in the days of actors under contract, everybody would eat together in the Commissary. It did not matter whether you were an A-list actor, or a newly hired administrative assistant, everybody went to the same place for food.

I have spoken to a few people who had very similar experiences getting hired at Universal, and others whose experiences were unrecognizable from my own. The important thing for everyone applying to work for Disney or Universal is this: the first thing you need to be able to answer for yourself is what you want to do within the company. The secondary question, of course, is how to get yourself there.

While I will offer advice that references theme parks, entertainment resort destinations, and cruise lines in general, much of my career track and growth was at Disney. As a result, my primary focus will be on going to work for the Mouse.

First things first, ask yourself why. Why do you want to work for Disney, Universal or any resort operation? Make sure you can answer that question. It can be as simple as needing a job or something more nuanced. Building your interview preparation around why will help you to have a successful interview or audition. You then expand your questioning a little more. Where? Are you okay with travel, with relocation? What would you like to do, and what skills do you bring? Is this a career move for you, or something to kill time? Let's look at these questions one by one.

My *WHY* was simple: I had to be part of the Magic. Maybe yours is the same. Maybe not. You might be looking for experience, a launching pad career, or a paycheck. Maybe you have always wanted to work around marine mammals. Perhaps the rough-edged vibe of Universal Studios holds more appeal and more fits your personality. Maybe you just need a job. All these reasons are equally as valid.

Considering *WHERE* you would like to work is difficult without also considering what you'd like to be doing, but there are a couple of cursory things to consider about location. First of all, if you know that you'd like to work for Disney but don't think you can move to an area that supports a park, consider working for a Disney satellite operation like the Disney Store. Working at a satellite operation still comes with the bonus of being a cast member, which gets you access to Disney's international hiring and transfer protocols.

Maybe you want to work on a Disney Cruise Line (DCL) ship instead? Or perhaps you'd prefer a job at one of the Disney Vacation Club (DVC) resorts like Aulani, Hilton Head, or Vero Beach. No matter what operation you set your sights on, make sure you learn about the specifics of that location. More likely than not, you will find a way to plug yourself in.

When considering *WHAT* you'd like to do as a Disney employee, the possibilities can seem endless. Both Disney and Universal have over three thousand job classifications, not including approved vendor lists and third-party partners. That is three thousand different opportunities for you to fit in with your interests and skill set. As a result, figuring out what you have an interest in doing is a valid starting point when trying to enter the world of theme park work. So consider: which positions and roles appeal to you? Are there any particular jobs you think you would be a good fit for? A great fit? Even if you don't think you can land the theme park job of your dreams immediately, consider other positions that will allow you to get a foot in the door. If you need to find your way through the house, it's always better to be inside, versus outside, knocking on the door.

An old friend of mine knew he wanted to join a stunt show at one of the Disney parks. Landing a stuntman gig for Disney, however, can be difficult as a starting position, so he did the next best thing: he got hired into costuming. After a while, he requested a transfer to the costuming department for the stunt show where he wanted to perform. Once there, he studied, he learned, and eventually he auditioned for and got cast in the part he had been eyeing from the very start of his journey.

Then there's Jon. I met Jon on a flight to Atlanta. When this gentleman found out I worked for Disney, he could barely keep himself in his seat, he was that excited. And trust me, I understood. For the rest of the flight, he peppered me with questions. He wasn't a fan of his current job and seemed to be looking for a way out. It seemed like a classic case of corporate malaise affecting a man who had been sold a different bill of goods than was advertised when he first started his career. We exchanged contact information and stayed in touch.

Jon needed a change. It was more than not being happy with what he was doing. I got the impression that it was either make the change or sacrifice his sanity. He convinced his family to relocate to Orlando, and Jon applied for a job at Disney, where he got hired into merchandise. This full-grown adult and father of two, who did not have a single day of retail experience, was undeterred in his new position. He didn't care what he did so long as he was working for Disney. I got that one-thousand percent.

Over time, other opportunities within the company presented themselves to him. In his short time with Disney, Jon passed through four different roles in two different lines of business. Like me, he didn't really care what he was doing for Disney if he could just get his foot in the door. Recently, he reached out to me and shared the good news: his temporary assignment as a manager in park ops had changed to a statused assignment - he was now a full-time manager. He could not have been happier, and I could not have been happier for him. I knew Jon had been a leader in his previous career, and he relished the fact that at Disney, he could truly lead again, and be happy doing it.

Another friend of mine, Angie, had a similar journey at Universal. Angie always gleefully admits to being a fantasy nerd. Her job at Islands of Adventure at the Lost Continent was right up her alley, but when Universal announced that Hogwarts was coming, Angie knew she had to be a part of the opening team. If The Lost Continent was her wheelhouse, then Hogwarts was her ship. A year after the land of Harry Potter opened, I asked Angie if she still enjoyed working there.

"This place is like its own theme park," Angie said and grinned mischievously. "We *actually* get to make magic every single day."

I knew it was a good-natured rib at Disney, but I didn't mind. The employees at this wizardly world had actual magic wands that appeared to create actual magic. The technology behind the sorcerous whimsy at Universal's Hogsmeade is first rate, but that technology means nothing without people like Angie to give the park life.

That land *is* almost like its own theme park. There's a vested ownership to the place that I haven't seen replicated at any other park, anywhere in the world. The first time I wandered aimlessly through Diagon Alley, I saw Universal team members walking around, talking to guests, and bringing the world of Harry Potter to life with every, "No, dear, it's *levi-OO-sa*".

Now let's consider your *SKILLS*. What could you bring to the table of a theme park or resort? The Disney corporation is, first and foremost, a corporation of entertainers and more. If you're a dancer or singer, you have a strong shot getting in through traditional audition avenues. If you have experience as a specialty act, you can submit a reel to the respective contract acts department. If you're a stunt performer, a gymnast, an ice skater, a musician - opportunities abound. The Walt Disney World resort in Orlando, Disneyland in California, and international Disney parks all have associated resorts that require people who can sing, play musical instruments, have a band, juggle, or entertain in other ways. The Disney Cruise Line is one of many touring Disney productions (because the ships travel and reposition with their crew) that relies heavily on such entertainers.

Remember that Disney employees are called cast members. Walt Disney himself, who founded the company with his brother Roy, had a strong entertainment background. As Disneyland was being built in 1955, many of his Imagineers and executives came from the television and film industry. No matter whether someone's role is onstage (anywhere guests could be present) or backstage (anywhere out of direct sight of the guests), Disney employees are part of a cast, they have a role. Using such nomenclature serves as a reminder that every part of the Disney operation is uniquely oriented to provide guests with the best show experience possible. The job title thus becomes part of an expectation alignment, and just like Broadway tours, and other entertainment productions, Disney seeks out the best and most qualified people to cast for roles in their parks, resorts, and cruise line operations.

Similarly, Universal represents every aspect of entertainment that Disney does. They put on live shows, stunt shows, parades, and character meet and greets. Like Disney, Universal parks have a global presence. Universal also hosts its world-renowned Halloween

Horror Nights, an event that requires a cast of thousands every single night. This separate ticketed event provides an excellent opportunity for aspiring theme park workers to get a foot in the door with Universal. They also have a wonderful partnership with Loews Hotels, who manage every resort on the Orlando property and are always in need of people to fill entertainment roles, regular and seasonal.

As you can see, opportunities at theme parks are not few or far between. If you're just looking to get your foot in the door of the entertainment industry, consider simply making an appointment or walking into the casting building in Orlando. I've known plenty of people who start out as a Disney Cast Member and end up on Broadway and on tour; many of the people I worked with at Universal's stunt shows later found roles as actors, action choreographers, and second unit directors in film and television.

No matter what, it's important to keep in mind that your career path at a theme park will rarely be the straightest or most direct one, but most people who stay with Disney or Universal for the long haul never consider leaving. I know that I celebrated the fact that I was there daily, even as months turned into years… which turned into decades.

Decisions have been made and you know which role to go for. One of the simplest ways to get an in with Disney, if you are qualified, is through the College Program (CP) or the International College Program (ICP). As the name suggests, this method is open to current college or university students, and for those close to graduating and newly graduated. I wish I had known about this program the first time I was applying for a job at Disney.

When recruiting for CP or ICP, Disney recruiters visit campuses throughout the country and the world, looking for people seeking opportunities with Disney. This style of recruitment looks to fill countless positions across dozens of different lines of business, including admin support, custodial, entertainment, food and beverage, and country ambassadors. Certain universities even offer students work or college credit for their time at Disney. For college students, it is truly the best of both worlds. Not only are you being paid decently, but you're also learning a great deal about the industry from an entertainment giant. Additionally, Disney works out all the arrangements on behalf of their CP and ICP recruits, including transportation to and from the Disney park for the program.

If you are participating in one of these college programs, it is important to be aware that there are additional guidelines surrounding living accommodations and work schedules that you will be expected to follow. Attendance is one example. While Disney's park and resort employee attendance policies are some of the most forgiving that I have ever come across - you have to miss a considerable amount of time before the topic of company separation is even approached, and leading up to that, managers always reach out for welfare checks - it would be remiss of me not to emphasize that Disney takes empowering responsibility very seriously. When I was an entertainment manager for one of the parks, I unfortunately had to reach out to an ICP cast member and inform her that her time with the program was being terminated due to excessive absences. I was upset - so upset that I felt on the verge of throwing up after the call was made. But after reviewing her record, my fellow leader and I saw that she had been giving a plentitude of chances and had received a few wellness checks by this point, to no avail of changing her attendance record.

I share this story because it's important to set personal expectations before doing a college program with Disney. Yes, the program offers an exceptional opportunity to meet, work with, and live among fellow college students from all over the world. Of course, time to socialize, make friends, and even party is foundational to the overall experience. But Disney will always require people to show up for the role they were given. Remember, the job/role is the first and primary reason a CP or ICP participant is recruited.

If you find yourself participating in a CP or ICP program, focus on doing your absolute best in the role you're given. The College Program has been (and continues to be) a foot in the door for tens of thousands of people looking to get a start in the entertainment industry of theme parks and resorts. Many CP students and interns seek opportunities above and beyond the initial job description of their program. Attendance and performance are just some ways to shine during your program semester, and you are constantly being evaluated. It's like an every-day audition for Disney. If you are remotely considering the prospect of applying for a full-time position after college, it's important to give every single day on the job your very best.

It's always a bittersweet moment as the program semester comes to an end, reminding outstanding CP and ICP Cast Members that "Disney will be here" when they graduate. Disney always likes to say we're a family, and it's never fun to see such bright, shining orbs of light leave the company, even temporarily. Sometimes these conversations are necessary because the CP or ICP is thinking about not leaving. I've had more than one conversation where I encouraged the CP cast member to finish their degree, and then come back, if they chose to.

Universal is similar. While they do not have an equivalent of Disney's College Program, internships abound. As there is no specific hiring window, there are always plenty of positions in need of filling. Internships, offered in all lines of business at the parks and resorts, are great first steps to getting into the company.

Other than college programs and internships, there are a few key entry points into the theme park and resort industry. Working as a third party-vendor can be a great way to get your foot in the door as an Operating Participant (OP) new hire. In such a position, you first must meet the standard criteria for the third-party company, then additionally align with the same Disney expectations applicable to working in all their parks and resorts. New OP hires, like all cast members, go through Traditions, so there is still a sprinkling of pixie dust for everybody, no matter which employment door they walk through. Universal also has the option of going through a third-party to potentially become part of the team.

As mentioned earlier, Loews hotels have partnered with Universal Orlando operations pretty much since the first park opened. If you have an interest in hospitality and still want to be part of the Universal magic, consider applying for a job at one of these resort hotels. Even if they aren't inside the parks, these places are vibrant attractions in and of themselves. Think of the shopping and entertainment districts, like Universal City Walk. Just as with Disney's hotels, the Loews hotels have additional appeal, such as dining and entertainment offerings not exclusive to those staying on the resort's property.

As you're entering this next chapter of your life, remember that casting processes and hiring protocols are flexible. Walt Disney was fond of saying that Disneyland would always be changing, that even the trees as they grew would alter the look and feel of the park. "Disneyland will never be completed," he's known for stating. "It will continue to grow as long as there is imagination left in the world." This evolving adaptability colors every aspect of the industry in general. To that end, there is more than one path by which to secure a job interview with a Disney park or resort. These include online applications, in person walk-ins, or cast member and current employee referrals.

On the other hand, the process with Universal usually starts online. You typically have to set up a career profile through the Universal or NBC Universal career site. If you have a degree in hospitality, business administration, or similar, be sure to indicate that experience, as well as your *why* for pursuing that educational path. Keep in mind that having a degree is not always enough to land you a new position. Explain how your degree will benefit the operation and share how you can apply your education to become a valuable asset to a theme park team. If you have any internship or work experience, make that known as well. Did you choose an education in hospitality because you have a passion for helping people and operations grow, or because the idea of servant leadership resonates with you? Do you simply like people? Let the person you are interviewing know the specifics and shine with your personal details.

If you don't have a college degree, don't worry. Tell the recruiter how big a fan you are of the respective park and its associated company. Demonstrate that you know, understand and believe in its culture. Highlight how helping people is a passion of yours and find examples from your lived experience to back up your points. Convey your willingness to work nights, weekends, and holidays in order to ensure guests leave happier than they arrived. Creating special moments can be more rewarding than experiencing them for yourself. If you are bubbling with enthusiasm, by all means, let it show. Express your excitement about the company and its culture in your own words and dig deep to share your beliefs and values at the same time, focusing particularly in how the two align. Your sincerity will shine, and at the end of the day, these companies care more about finding someone who will click with the culture and community than someone with three degrees. Remember, they do the training. For most entry level positions, a blank slate with personality is exactly what they are looking for.

Maybe the ocean is calling you, and you want to work on the Disney Cruise Line (DCL). In that case, double down on your research. Make sure you understand the expectations of working on what is essentially a floating resort; there will be a variety of expectations you will encounter that wouldn't be relevant on a land-based role. Where you might think a ten-hour shift at a park is a long day, you can expect to work anywhere from fourteen to sixteen hours a day on a boat. When you work on land and you finish your shift, you go home. At sea, when your shift is done, you go to your berth or meet some friends on deck, but you're still on the ship. If someone needs you, you'll be called. You can also expect to work seven days a week, helping guests leave or reboard the ship in the mornings and afternoons, rehearsing for shows if you're part of a stage production, or leading training sessions if you're an officer. While you'll get good at finding pockets of time to shoehorn rest and personal obligations, a full day to get caught up on laundry or binge watch your favorite show? On a cruise ship, such a thing is extraordinarily rare to come by.

Even the hiring process for working on a DCL ship is different. You start by submitting an online application or audition reel, depending on the role you have in mind. If the recruiter or hiring manager like what they see, they will reach out to schedule an appointment. After the interview, you can expect to learn the next steps of the hiring process, whether that is a second interview, an audition or call back, or, in the case of people applying for senior leadership roles, a stepped interview process.

For officer designated roles on the ships, expect a multi-tiered interview process, where each one is different from the previous. Background checks for DCL positions are more intensive than they are for land-based park jobs, as are the medicals. To land the role, this much is certain: you must be all in physically and mentally. Your work cycle is typically a six-month contract, where you spend four months on the ship and two months off. The bonus is that when you're off the ship, you're not working at all. You won't be called to come in or expected to respond to any issues that come up. When you're not on the ship, you can be entirely disconnected from your work life. Another perk to consider as a officer is that your room and board are entirely taken care of. Someone else is doing not only your cooking, but your food shopping. Gratis laundry service is also available to certain crew members with officer designations. As a DCL crew member, you're privy to many of the same conveniences as the guests are, though the benefits will change depending on the role.

A friend of mine went to work on a cruise ship, first as a performer then as a contract act. He told me it gave him a chance to do what he loved while he decided what to do next. He didn't have a house or apartment, so mortgage and utilities weren't a concern for him. Instead, he worked six and a half year on DCL ships and used his time off to travel and stay with friends. At the end of this run, he had one heck of a nest egg with which to buy a home and begin the next chapter of his life. Now, he has his own TV show and twenty acres of rolling farmland in Tennessee. I would say he stuck his landing.

Working on a cruise ship is not for everyone, but for those who mesh with the lifestyle, it's an opportunity unlike anything else in the world. On one of my DCL cruises, I recognized one of the crew members while dining in Animator's Palate. Kirk had just come through a DCL Traditions class, and as I watched him running food, looking like he had everything under control, I sensed he was still trying to figure out how things worked. At one point in the evening, he looked over and gave me a smile of recognition. As things settled and guests began to trickle out, I called Kirk over to ask how he was doing. He came over and nodded that things were good, but I could see him questioning if he'd ever be able to get a handle on his many responsibilities. He said it was a lot of information on top of a lot of information, and I thought of the expression "drinking from a fire hose". I reminded him how rigorous the DCL hiring process was, that someone looked at *him* and saw something great, something they knew the ship would be incomplete without. He nodded and thanked me for the reminder. When Kirk melted away to wrap his closing and side work, I noticed a couple at the next table, smiling and looking at me like they were in on the secret. In a way, I guess they were. They had been given a chance to look behind the curtain, get a glimpse at the vast network of interpersonal relationships and support systems that go into ensuring their experience on the ship is one of a lifetime.

Disney's vessels, with their elegant and evocative lines suggestive of early 1900s ocean liners, are enough to make one emotional. When you report for your first role, the first time you're on board and your ship pulls away from port, playing a song steeped in nostalgia like "When You Wish Upon a Star"? That sensation you get? That's magic of another level, pure pixie dust.

Perhaps your heart is set on getting cast in a Disney or Universal show. If so, then it might be time to start preparing yourself in anticipation of getting cast for the stage. Consider the types of stage show roles you're interested in, and with your eye on the prize, start honing your skills. Do you have a martial arts background? Some characters inhabiting the Star Wars Universe (such as Kylo-Ren and Darth Maul) employ martial arts movement in their on-stage performances. A gymnastics background can be similarly put to good use. How about your acting and dance background? Do you sing? Both Universal and Disney are known for casting singers who can move and dancers who can sing, even if there's an emphasis on one over the other. In other cases, as with Epcot's "Guardians of the Galaxy: Cosmic Rewind" live show, cast members must do both equally well. Even if these requirements seem intimidating, don't rule yourself out if you don't think you have the performance proficiency of a Broadway triple threat (someone who can act, dance, and sing). I've seen casting exceptions made in plenty of cases where someone shows up with obvious talent and an abundance of positivity. Even though they might not have a full range of skills at the audition, the casting team decides to take a chance on them.

Additionally, bear in mind that Universal and Disney aren't the only theme park operators in the central Florida corridor. There is also Sea World, Legoland a little further west, and Busch Gardens further west still. All these companies host live shows and character meet and greets. They also all offer some version of holiday entertainment and will cast specifically for those events - particularly Halloween and December celebrations. Auditioning for seasonal shows is an excellent way to get yourself on the radar as a performer and potentially catch the interest of the talent casting team associated with the larger operation. This is because the same talent casting teams do the work of casting, regardless the time of year or show being mounted. Places that are not considered theme parks, per se, provide seasonal offerings that require actors and other talent. Many resorts get in on the holiday fun by providing seasonal offerings, both to on-site guests and those visiting.

You can sign up to receive email notifications for nearly all the opportunities listed above. These are generally initiated by Disney or Universal, but colleges and casting directors will frequently pick up these notifications and disseminate them, too. I recommend finding your way to an official website, like the Disney Careers site or the Universal Jobs website, and sign up for email blasts. I promise, it'll be worth the little bit of inbox space.

A word of warning. There are plenty of companies that pass themselves off as casting agents or facilities. They will claim to be conducting auditions for Disney and Universal. They may go so far as saying they are official representatives of the companies and will borrow Walt Disney's scripts and typesets to advertise casting for Disney, and feature stock images of Halloween Horror Nights for Universal. In almost every case, these companies will not offer you anything that you cannot actively go after yourself. They rarely have special connections or avenues to the parks or resorts. I'd recommend steering clear of such agencies and businesses. Be especially wary of any audition that wants to charge you, or that makes themselves out as a training school to help you land a part. The business model for these is simple: you come to the audition, and no matter how well you do, they tell you they can work with you and their acting school will add the finishing touches for what you need. Don't buy it, figuratively and literally.

Both Disney and Universal maintain their own creative talent casting departments and never charge a fee to audition for one of their productions. If someone tries to charge you a fee, no matter how they justify it, turn around and leave. Always do your due diligence.

Once you find an entertainment role and decide to go after it, pay attention to the details and requirements for that specific audition. For example, if you're auditioning for a singing position, identify the style of music you will be expected to come in having prepared. In most cases, the music will already be written and arranged, unless you are auditioning to be part of an opening cast for a new production. It goes without saying that you shouldn't show up to a "Voices of Liberty" audition with a piece of pop music - the style of this group is acappella: some pieces may require belting and modulation, but typically not vibrato. Likewise, don't bring your folk music ballads to a "Guardians of the Galaxy Dance Party" type audition. These high energy musical shows require pop range, rock control, and associated choreography that will be indicated in the audition notice. If they are mounting a staple or familiar show, like "The Rocky Horror Picture Show" - which Universal has done for HHN - in addition to doing the previously mentioned, be very familiar with any of the roles you might be auditioning for.

The audition notices for any show or production are clear and precise enough that the auditionee shouldn't stumble across any surprises on the day of the audition itself.

Maybe someone has told you that you look like a Disney Princess (something that I - and this may or may not surprise you - have never been told in my entire life). In this case, Disney character auditions might be the place for you. These roles have strict height and profile requirements, and unless you are the extraordinary ingénue who can be the media face for one of the princesses, not meeting the height requirements will get you a courteous, "Thank you," and could end the audition for you then and there. Having said that, I've seen plenty of instances where the casting directors have asked someone to stick around because they have something else in mind for them. This applies to the rest of the Disney character roles as well.

Having a good singing voice and resembling a famous Disney character could land you a face role in a stage production. Universal will frequently cast people who meet the height, build, and musical talent requirements for certain roles. Think of "The Blues Brother's" show at Universal Studios. You don't have to be a look-alike to get cast, but they are looking for people who look more or less like they belong. Universal also frequently casts for talent that looks like, sounds like, and possess similar mannerisms to individuals like Marilyn Monroe, Betty Boop, the cast of Scooby-Doo, The Avengers, The Marx Brothers, Lucille Ball, or Schwarzenegger's Terminator. Similarly, Disney will also look for look-alikes for their pantheon of face characters.

New shows are always being developed, so be sure to communicate your skill sets on your résumé and in person. Just because you don't see a Tiana or Moana show yet doesn't mean there isn't one in the works. It can take a show months or years to mount, and talent casting is always looking beyond the scope of the show they're currently auditioning. I've been asked to stick around after an audition plenty of times, because another show was in the works.

With a strong athletics, gymnastics, or martial arts background, you might be entertaining the idea of auditioning for a stunt show. Some shows require you to send in a reel first. If you don't have one ready, they're easy enough to make. If you have a stunt background, get a few friends together and film some basic choreography. It doesn't have to be anything longer then 20 to 30 seconds, just something that highlights your skill set. If you're trained in gymnastics or parkour, get footage that captures your ability to do basic things like tumbles, somersaults, and flips. Likewise for martial arts. This footage should showcase your skills; it doesn't have to be polished because the people conducting the audition understand you may not be coming in with a lot of show business experience. They just want to see you demonstrating the necessary skill set that can be plugged into whatever it is they have in mind for you. In other words, they're looking for a foundation that they can build upon and mold for the show they're casting.

Somewhere on the audition notification they'll tell you what to wear. If it says to wear comfortable clothes, do that. It's going to be pretty difficult to bang out ten to twenty proper pull-ups if you show up wearing a form-fitting dress shirt. There's a strong chance stunt show auditions will do a preliminarily physical agility test. Finding the guy who looks like the perfect Indiana Jones doesn't mean anything if he doesn't have the upper body strength to do two pull-ups. Some auditions will ask you to demonstrate your ability using a tumble track, tumble mats, a mini tramp, or even ask you to do high falls. Make sure you are highly proficient in these physical skills before going in. There's a saying in the stunt side of the industry: don't take the call if you can't do the fall. I cannot emphasize that enough. If you have any doubts about your ability to perform a certain stunt, don't let it hold you back from the audition, but be up front about it when asked. I've seen people whose enthusiasm trumped their skill set get cast in a show. Casting directors know these skills can be trainable, and it's better to honest about your capabilities than attempt something outside your wheelhouse and injure yourself.

Word about stuff like that gets out and can make it hard to get hired as a physical performer in the future. No matter what, be agreeable, willing to learn, and act professionally. Show up with the confidence of knowing you've done the trick, kick, or high fall you're about to demonstrate hundreds if not thousands of times already. 99 out of 100 times the audition team has seen enough to know what they're looking for and whether or not you can do it.

For every type of audition, make sure you warm up first. It may seem like obvious, common-sense advice, but I can't tell you how many seasoned performers have gotten injured because their bodies weren't properly prepared. Whether you're singing, dancing, sword fighting, demonstrating your Drunken Money, or jumping off a building, make sure the muscles you're about to show off are ready to perform for the occasion. And hydrate. Bring water, tea, whatever it is you like to drink (so long as it's not alcoholic - something I've seen brought to a particularly unsuccessful audition before). I cannot overstate how important hydration is in any audition context. Double down on the hydration if the audition is outside, in Florida.

The most important thing I can emphasize and promote is a positive attitude. Over time, height requirements for various roles have varied. People who have stumbled through a couple of choreography steps have been cast over former Broadway dancers because they brought exceptional positivity and energy to the audition. I have seen it happen. The minute you step into an audition building, everyone will be watching you. You never know if the assistant working the door will be seated in the director's chair later. I've been in auditions where someone in the waiting room was actually on the casting side of the production. Be courteous to everyone. Some of the folks you run into at this audition are probably associated with shows you may audition for in the future. If you think your parents have a long memory about something you did wrong, the entertainment industry has a memory like a dozen elephants. It never forgets.

Not just a work and entertainment hack: be civil and courteous to everyone.

Here's something I've heard from casting directors before, but it still took me a while working within the industry to fully internalize: the casting team is made up of people who *want* you to do well. They *want* to like you, and they *want* you to be exactly what they're looking for - even if sometimes they're not entirely sure of what that is. The notion of an adversarial relationship between casting directors and auditionees can be a dangerous mindset to have when starting or flowing through the process. In almost all cases, casting directors themselves began as actors in stage shows, just like you (this applies across the board, throughout the entertainment industry). It's possible they've even performed the very show you're auditioning for. They get it, they understand the nerves and know what it feels like to get up there, feeling pressure to be exactly what it takes for that callback. Chances are, they've felt the self-doubt, the "Am I actually prepared or good enough?" internal dialogue. And they're rooting for you.

For many shows, the audition is the easy part. Afterwards comes the callback, the casting, the costume fittings, and the rehearsals. Sometimes you can get as far as the fitting before the show gets shelved, and you're back to square one. Sometimes, you will be halfway through the rehearsal process…and they rewrite the entire show. That's entertainment, and it's happened to me more than once. You learn to make your peace with it and you learn to go with the flow. Sometimes, the casting team will like you so much that they'll still onboard and train you as a sub for other shows.

Remember, there's a strong chance one of those casting directors is looking beyond the scope of the immediate show they're preparing. Every time you audition, the casting will be considering what other shows you might be a good fit for. The same cross utilization that happens while working in operations also happens in entertainment. Countless park performers will work more than one stage in a day. Don't be surprised if the Dapper Dan you saw at Magic Kingdom in the morning happens to be on the "Hoop Dee Doo Revue" stage that same evening. It happened for me more times than I can count, where I would race across the park to get from one show to another. Many times, I would travel from Disney to Universal, and vice versa, to do shows in the same day. Universal Studios to Pirates? No problem. Disney to Sleuths? Sure. Singers, actors, stunt people, and character performers all increase their value by becoming versatile in multiple stage roles. Every time you audition, you demonstrate that valuable adaptability. Knowing more than one role on several stages for me was nothing compared to some of the individuals who were cast in every show across four parks and across town.

But if you don't get cast, try not to take it personally. There are always more people showing up for a role than there are roles to fill, and if you don't get the part you want, take the opportunity to ask for feedback. Then you can adjust for your next audition. Like I said, the casting directors want you to do well, and they'll be happy to offer feedback. Taking their advice can show that you take notes on your performance constructively and that you're serious about getting cast. I had a Casting Director once tell me the reason they put me in a show was because I kept asking for feedback. He told me I was the only actor who persisted in asking for feedback. Don't get me wrong. That can sometimes be difficult, especially when you know you're not moving on to a callback. Remember: any kind of feedback is an opportunity to learn and build. Ask for it and apply the notes given.

For those who are passionate about working in entertainment but are shy or uncomfortable interacting with thousands of strangers every day, every single stage operation needs a backstage crew to carry it. Pop up shows are the same. These teams are responsible for everything including production, training, documentation, costumes, and safety. Some of the most incredible people I've ever had the good fortune to work with were part of the backstage crew. Working behind the scenes makes you no less a cast member, no less a team member, no less a part of the magic behind the mission. It's not an exaggeration to say that life and death decisions are managed from the tech booth.

If you're looking for a leg up into the theme park and resort world, I'd recommend doing some extra homework. Watch the show you'd eventually like to perform. If it's not possible to do so live, I promise there are dozens of online videos of the show you've set your sights on. The premise is no different from researching any other company you might interview for - knowing expectations ahead of time means that you have a better idea of what the casting directors want. You can go into the audition with a smile, thinking to yourself that no matter what is asked of you, you'll be able to reply, "I'm ready, and I can do that."

No matter how you look at it though, there's always going to be a degree of inscrutable subjectivity and luck when trying to get on stage. I remember when a friend of mine from the character department auditioned for the Indiana Jones stunt double role at Disney. He had the look, the height, the high fall skills, the stunt fighting, and the whip cracking. He didn't make it past the first audition stage, and when he asked one of the members of the casting team why, he was simply told, "You don't look like Indiana Jones." Fast forward to casting doubles and media-trained actors for Star Wars. The team from Lucasfilm had first right of refusal over any actors vying for the principal parts of Luke, Leia, and Han Solo. The production team had a clear picture of what they wanted for each role. Guess who George Lucas himself picked as the number one casting spot for Han. It was indeed my friend, the one who didn't look like Indy to the casting team. It was Harrison Ford in both roles, but somehow, he looked like one version of the actor behind the character over the other.

To this day we still don't get it, but in its own way, even that makes sense for two reasons. The first is certain attributes of a well-known character maybe more important than the actual look itself. Body mechanics and movement can be taught, but not always. The second reason is how curvy a straight line is. Nothing about my time at Disney was ever simple or straightforward. When I started to work for Disney, I was part of the attractions operations team for "Inside the Magic". Basically, Disney MGM Studios (as the park was called at the time) was a working motion picture and production facility. "Inside the Magic" pulled back the curtain to demonstrate how the movies were made. Guests watched segments from several blockbuster films, then got to see how the special effects and other behind-the-scenes features were created on the soundstage.

During this time, I became friends with several of the performers in the "Indiana Jones Epic Stunt Spectacular" show in the way you might expect. During the show, there was an interactive part where an audience member is picked out of the crowd. Any time I went to see the show as a guest, come this interactive part, I would scream like a raving lunatic to get their attention. After a while, I only had to stand up, wave my arms, shout once, and they would recognize and pick me.

One of the trainers I became friends with taught me basic stunt work to develop my coordination, and once satisfied, he taught me the choreography of the titular Indiana Jones role. I learned the entire show and went to the audition. The casting director at the time knew I had learned the role, and everyone believed I was going through the audition process as a formality. However, during the audition, the show's stunt coordinator leaned over, and I watched him point at my headshot and whisper, "He's not ready." The casting director quietly removed my photo and shuffled it into the larger pile of headshots that would be dismissed. I was devastated. I believed I was the perfect fit for the role, and I was certain it was my time.

After a couple weeks of licking my wounds and feeling pathetically sorry for myself, I learned Universal Studios was hosting auditions for "The Wild Wild Wild West Stunt Show". The audition requirements indicated that all I had to do, at least initially, was show up with a monologue. On the big day, I walked inside and signed my name on the roster. Then an assistant called us back a few at a time, and we performed our monologues. When it was my turn, I found myself facing a gentleman at the center of a table, with the most spectacular British accent I had ever heard. He introduced himself as Adrian, and he explained that he was an actor, but not from the stunt side of things. He said he knew exactly what he was looking for. After I performed Rowan Atkinson's "A Warm Welcome" (laughs, to my relief, coming in as expected), Adrian looked at me. He asked if I'd ever fallen off a horse.

"Not intentionally," I replied. I was too nervous to try to be funny, but Adrian laughed. Four people received callbacks, and I was one of them.

Sunday morning, I reported to Universal Studios, where security at the gate had my name. I drove in and parked behind the stage, where the second part of the audition would be held. I was the first one there. Even though the dress code for the second audition was jeans and boots, I added a western dress shirt to my look. I had no idea what I was in for this morning, and I wanted to keep making a good impression - at least with my wardrobe if with nothing else. Unintentionally, I had done something that would later become part of my auditioning routine: I dressed towards the part I was auditioning for. Years later, I showed up to an audition for a role set in a medical facility, wearing scrubs and a lab coat. I even made an ID for extra measure. I booked that role. Now I can actually say, "I'm not a medical professional but I've played one on TV."

The four of us who received callbacks were gathered from the green room and brought onto the stage, where Adrian greeted us. Also there to receive us was a horse

"Right," he asked. "Who's getting on first?"

I looked around. One guy started backing up, whether intentionally or not I still don't know. I do know that he had the unmistakable look of fear in his eyes. Another guy, in a perfectly normal voice, said, "Hell no. Remember what happened to Christopher Reeves?"

I waited a couple of seconds then piped up, "I'll go."

I walked over to the horse, checked the girth strap to see if it was cinched tight enough, and made sure the saddle was more or less centered on the horse's back. When I started to adjust the stirrups, one of the wrangler's told me to climb on and she would help with that afterwards. I got settled into the saddle, then took the reins and led the horse, named Cody, around in a small circle and came to a stop in front of Adrian.

"What would you like me to do?" I asked.

He smiled and said, "Walk him down to the other end of the stage and bring him back."

"That's it? Sure." I walked Cody across the stage, did a gentle lead when I got there, full circle, before coming back. There were a lot of things buried in the stage, fall pads and props and the like, but Cody knew the stage like the back of his hoof and eased around everything. When I returned to Adrian and the other auditionees, I stopped, slipping the reigns over the saddle horn. Adrien nodded his thanks, so I dismounted and handed Cody's reins to the wrangler.

As someone else approached the horse, Adrian told me, "Whether or not we cast you, you'll get a call this week."

I nodded. As noncommittal a response as I could have hoped for. I found out later that Adrian knew he wanted to cast me in the show as soon as he saw me on the horse. It wasn't that I was a great actor or an excellent equestrian; I had just showed up with a positive attitude and an eagerness to listen and learn.

I got the call later that week telling me they wanted me. I would be the last Brett Taylor hired for "The Wild Wild Wild West Stunt Show" while the stunt show still used horses (Universal would ultimately change the show to omit the animals, but that didn't happen for almost a decade). For now, I had joined the fellowship of Universal stunt team members who worked with horses. The most important thing I learned when working with animals was to pay attention to the horse and pay attention to the trainers. Assume that everyone else on the stage has been there longer than you. If you listen, you'll learn the tricks necessary to execute the show. If you fail to pay attention, you run the risk of getting injured.

I had been Brett Taylor for about three months when, during our post show meet and greet, the Disney stunt coordinator I recognized from my Indiana Jones audition came over. He was smiling.

"I always knew you could do it. You were almost there before, and I'm glad you didn't give up."

It was a peculiar feeling. At the time of my Disney audition, I was mad as hell at him for taking the Indiana Jones opportunity away from me. Now, I realized he had set me up for an opportunity that, due to my pretty extensive experience around horses, was much more in line with my practical and growing skill set at the time. I don't know how he knew, but I chalked it up to him being good at his job. Even though I never got to play Indiana Jones, landing the show at Universal meant that soon I would learn the Hitchcock show and the "Terminator" show. I would end up traveling the world, doing shows in other countries and other continents before ultimately finding my way back to Disney as part of the opening team for the "Lights Motors Action" stunt show.

The point of my story is simple: don't give up. Ever. The entertainment industry is going to test you, it's going to see how badly you want it, and that's true whether you're an actor, stuntman, audiobook narrator - you name it. When everyone sees the end result of red-carpet walks, celebrity, and international travel, it's easy to forget the energy, effort, sweat, blood, tears, and years it takes to get there. A life in entertainment demands everything you have. When you think you're all out, you just have to dig a little deeper to find more of the passion and dedication that started you down this path in the first place. Nothing happens overnight, but when it finally does, it is well worth it, especially when you have those around you who continue to support you.

A final thing to consider is optics. I know of no other industry in the world where you can show up for the exact same interview two days in a row with the exact same team, and get two different responses. The difference can be as simple as someone sleeping through their alarm, or not getting their cup of coffee, or getting an extra cup of coffee, or waking up to roses. Persistence and positivity will reward your efforts.

Maybe you're thinking "I don't dance, jump off of buildings, or have a hospitality degree." Perhaps you aren't interested in going into entertainment in the conventional sense but still want to work at a theme park or company that owns such a venue. The worlds of Disney and Universal can still be your oysters. If you feel like entertainment or showbiz aren't your calling, you don't have to dismiss the idea of working in attractions operations, resorts support, or in a role that may initially seem directionless or mundane. Remember, every theme park position teaches a skillset. One executive, Dan, retired from the Walt Disney World Park and Resort operation as a VP and now runs a successful consulting business. He started as a parking attendant with park operations. Disney Photo Imaging (DPI) will hire people with no photography experience, put them through the paces, and send them out to capture forever memories. These cast members go on to become trainers, managers, or even build their own boutique photography businesses. You can be a high-level executive and decide you've simply had enough of the corporate complex, or a recent high school graduate trying to find your footing in the professional world. Either way, you're in luck. Disney and Universal are almost always hiring.

From casting to Traditions to your first day on the theme park job, once Disney sees that you're a good fit for their culture and brand, they will ensure you get trained far above industry standard, regardless of your line of business. Disney is committed to providing you with tools and skills for ongoing development. Your managers will also be your mentors; company leaders will scout you for those next opportunities. Disney will always be an entertainment business, but as it turns out, they're also very much in the business of personal development. The unifying element between all these things is simple: relationship building.

If you want to pursue a career at Disney, inter-personal connections MUST be a priority. Connections lead to referrals, which can be an excellent first step to landing a role or position. It's likely that someone in your social circle has a connection to a current Disney or Universal employee. If not a friend, then a friend of a friend. Seek out these people and cultivate those relationships. These relationship-based referrals take on much greater significance once you've started working for a theme park operation than before.

My time with the Traditions team found me walking away with several dozen new friends. One of these new friends was Lloyd, an entertainment proprietor at Disney's Hollywood Studios. While Lloyd was technically my boss's boss, he was there for me from the start. At my Traditions reveal, when I learned for the first time that I was going to be teaching Disney Traditions, Lloyd was there with balloons, a disposable camera, and a big hug (which I desperately needed). After wrapping up my time with Traditions, Lloyd got wind that one of the Epcot teams needed an entertainment leader. While only a few of the Universal managers or proprietors knew my name at this point, I was getting great traction at Disney. Lloyd casually mentioned me to one of the Epcot team proprietors, then encouraged me to go interview.

Here's my next piece of advice: always say yes. Decisions that will affect your career track are frequently made long before you're even aware that there's a change taking place. It's like being a piece on a chessboard. I've found having my career steered for me in such a way was never a bad thing. Everyone I have spoken to at Disney and Universal agrees. The higher up the ladder you are, the more of the big picture you get to see. That's why it is smart and good to trust opportunities, like the one Lloyd gave me, when they come up.

At Epcot, I went to my first interview, which was with the proprietor of entertainment, Matt. During our conversation, I asked him how he found out about me, and he mentioned Lloyd. Matt told me how Lloyd emphasized how much passion for the company and its heritage I exhibited, and that I'd be a good addition to the team. He also mentioned Justin, who was part of my

Traditions team. Without asking, people were putting in a good word on my behalf. Matt offered me the position, and I said yes.

Justin, a fellow Traditions peer, would also be my boss on an ad hoc basis. At the time I was brought onboard Matt's team, Justin had been pulled for another project and would be gone for the day. Any salaried manager could have filled in for him, but Justin knew me and my abilities from Traditions. Even though I was a new hire, I essentially became the managerial point of contact for the entire park while Justin was away. It is for reasons like this I cannot emphasize the importance of relationship building enough. As I have said before, people at Disney and Universal become your family. They have not only the best interests of the company, but your best interests, at heart. They want you to succeed and are aware that the key to that success is to make sure you land the roles that are best suited to you, your skill sets, and your potential. At the same time, it's going to be your responsibility to seek out those resources through the relationships you cultivate. This will be at times uncomfortable, but stepping out of your comfort zone is how you grow.

Throughout this section, I've been mentioning Traditions. It keeps coming up because, for a new Cast Member, going through Traditions can be a major life event. As your first day on the Disney clock, Traditions feels like it flies by. Blink and you're taking a selfie in front of Disney University, blink again and you're studying your role assignment and muddling through paperwork, or pinning on a handsome new Disney name tag. Whether you're there as a College Program participant, a full-time employee, a part-time hire, a Casual Temporary, or a Disney Crew Line member, the magic is the same. The reason why I mention Traditions can be a major life event in one's Disney career? If you ask somebody who went through traditions a year ago or 10 years ago, in many cases, they remember the facilitators, and the experience itself. That will make them smile. The feeling is more than nostalgic.

Walking into Disney University to sign in before heading up to your home room is a moment filled with anticipation and energy. Once in the room, you'll find your "Welcome to Disney" folder and the "Disney Look" guidebook among a host of other pamphlets waiting to be perused on the table. After your Traditions class, you're a fully-fledged cast member, vested, empowered and ready to become part of the next generation of storytellers.

When talking about your journey and your goals regarding working for Universal, Disney or any theme park operation, resort, or entertainment destination, you hold the keys to the kingdom. You can sing, dance, do acrobatics, or stunt ride off into so many sunset horizons. You can write, direct, choreograph, produce, and partner. No matter where you are, no matter what you are doing, you are part of a team and teamwork does indeed makes the dream work. The opportunities are there and yours to ask for. It simply falls on you to make clear that you understand the culture, have something to bring to the operation, and are ready to make magic and create happiness. First and foremost, bring your inner light, your positive outlook, and your sincerity when you show up to interview. Not only will you blow your audience away, but you will leave them wondering what took you so long to show up in the first place.

I'm including a list of links to various Disney and Universal programs and hiring platforms, and every attempt has been made to ensure these are up to date. However, these companies are always modifying their hiring procedures. This includes creating new websites and landing pages and removing others, so there's no guarantee these links will remain active for any length of time. Regardless, I hope they offer you a good starting point in your journey:

DISNEY LINKS*
https://jobs.disneycareers.com/disney-programs

https://profile.disneyauditions.com/people/sign_in?
locale=en

https://jobs.disneycareers.com/auditions

https://jobs.disneycareers.com/search-jobs

https://disneycastingscout.com/

UNIVERSAL LINKS*
https://jobs.universalparks.com

https://jobs.universalparks.com/universal-creative/

https://jobs.universalparks.com/job-search-results/

https://jobs.universalparks.com/auditions/

SIX FLAGS LINKS*

https://jobs.sixflags.com/

https://www.sixflags.com/

(*all links active as of publishing)

SO...YOU WORK AT A THEME PARK

In the previous section, you probably learned more than you needed to know about the various avenues of entry into the world of theme parks, notably Disney and Universal. In terms of information intake, it can be less like drinking from a water fountain and more like having a firehose aimed straight at your face. But even with everything that I provided in the previous section based on my own experiences, there's always more to learn through your own research. Such independent research is invaluable for the world of theme park work, where hiring practices change, new positions are added and others eliminated, and processes are always evolving. Certain personal perspectives are interpreted differently based on our individual priorities. What is important to me may be less so to you. We all have a different punch list of non-negotiables, but certain things should remain the same, like opportunity.

SAY YES.

Here we are. You did that research, you prepared, and now you're a team member, cast member, or both! You've unlocked the next level, so what's now?

First of all, celebrate your success. You got through the interview, passed the audition and callback, or negotiated a tiered series of leadership casting calls and selection committees. You were vetted, went through background checks and pre-employment checks, perhaps you were even confronted with a comprehensive medical check. After all that, you made it. You got hired. Cue the celebratory musical fanfare. You got the job, and you got more than a job. Whether you now find yourself the new employee of a theme park, traveling production, entertainment resort, or a floating Disney show at sea, you have become part of the magic.

You received an email or letter detailing your next steps, and then your first day starts, appropriately enough, with your day-one theme park orientation. As I mentioned in the previous section, whether you've been hired by Disney or Universal, this will be no ordinary orientation - which is only fitting, considering that these are no ordinary companies. During Traditions, you learn about the various backgrounds of the Tradition facilitators who will be teaching the class. You will also learn about the people seated at the table with you. You may discover some of them left Disney only to return; you'll meet others from every job imaginable, all who left to fulfill a lifelong dream of getting to call Mickey Mouse their boss. Think about it: lawyers and laymen, people from every ivory tower or blue collar walk of life chose to leave those worlds, so they could be sitting next to you in the House of the Mouse.

With great fondness, I recall both Tradition experiences. Having left Disney when my live entertainment and film career started to take off, I got to go through Disney orientation again. I very much looked forward to that. When you go through Traditions, you'll get it. My facilitators from my first Traditions experience are as memorable as the second one. One of them had started in attraction operations, and eventually became an Imagineer. The other started in food and beverage, and eventually moved to Disney University, where she designed and created instructional and training content. I would reconnect with her years later, when I would call Disney University home during my Traditions year.

During my second Disney go-round, I met someone who confessed that he had never felt so connected to a place until he got to wave a wand. One of my facilitators, who had been paying more in taxes than I was making in a year, left her C-suite position with a Fortune 500 company because she had felt like a hamster on a wheel. If she was working a job where the work came home with her, she wanted to look forward to it every day and know that she was making a difference. At Disney, teaching a flock of starry-eyed new recruits, that's just what she got to do. My other Traditions facilitator started life as a photographer who then opened a couple of barbecue restaurants because the man loves barbecue. The only thing he loved more, he told me, was Disney, and he didn't even realize it until his first ever trip to the Orlando resort in one of those classic "taking the family to Disney and never leaving" type stories. Eventually he wound up leaving the Disney organization and moving to the Carolinas where, you guessed it, he and his family opened another barbecue restaurant. It will be a lifelong question of what he loves more, Disney or brisket and baby back ribs.

Having gotten your foot in the door, alongside many others carried in by every walk of life, this section of the book will focus on the next steps for working within the industry. Specifically, here we will focus on movement and promotion within the Disney and Universal companies. These promotions, especially for tiered roles and positions with managerial responsibility, can happen internally within or across departments. For both companies, these promotions can take you anywhere. Movement can take place within the park or can relocate you to the other side of the country or halfway around the globe. As I list and go into greater detail about some of the ways in which you can grow your career and gain experience, there are plenty of opportunities beyond. For example, one temporary assignment, given to me, which might sound painfully boring, was asset tracking. No matter, the operation or industry, every company of a certain size has to do tracking and maintenance regarding technology. The park that I called home was no exception. Every few years it fell on departments to inventory and report their computers and technology peripherals. The decision had been made one year to have a single individual from any given department visit every location to track, identify, and log every asset. In the entertainment department, that individual was me. Before you get ahead of yourself, and wonder how bored out of my skull I was, let me share my own thoughts.

I thought I was going to be bored out of my skull. I found the experience to be anything but boring. I learned about different parts of the operation. I never knew existed, I learned about different locations and green rooms. I never knew existed, and I met a bunch of people I would never otherwise gotten to know. Who knew tracking down computers could be an enjoyable task-oriented activity? Not I.

There are numerous ways to gain traction as far as career growth and development are concerned. Whether you are in attractions operations, food and beverage, or entertainment, there is an opportunity with your name on it. These opportunities can come through committee assignments, by becoming a member of a specific team, employee cross-utilization, beta testing, a shadowing job, a transfer, or a temporary assignment. I'll go a little into what each of these entails.

Opportunities for Career Growth

Let's start with *COMMITTEES*. These can be part of a local line of business, a region of the park, or the entire park itself. In some cases, committees may encompass the entire property. They can run like focus groups, or they can be designed to come up with a couple of options to address anything from attendance to guest satisfaction measurements. Such committees usually include all kinds of employees, whether hourly or salaried. In these committees, you likely won't recognize the person sitting next to you, and round-robin introductions are how you start getting to know the others in the room.

You could be tapped to be part of a selection committee. These types of committees are for recipients of any service, merit, or performance-based award. Leadership committees are often made up of those who have experience in a given discipline for which selections are being made. I had the good fortune to be a part of various committees several times. I even served on the selection committee for the globally recognized TWDC Legacy award during the first and third years that it was instituted (I discovered after the fact that I hadn't been asked to serve during its second year because I myself had been nominated as a Legacy recipient!). My proprietor and manager both told me at the time how this was an incredibly special award, brand new to the company and global in nature. Doing my own research, I found out this award was the first time in the Walt Disney Company's history that a merit award would be treated for what it was - merit, no matter what park or resort you worked at. While each of the global Disney parks and resorts independently had some way of recognizing outstanding cast members, there was little uniformity between the awards. The Legacy Award would change that - whether awarded in Disneyland Paris, Walt Disney World, or Tokyo Disneyland, it proclaimed that the recipient was diligent in exceeding the same exacting worldwide company standards first demonstrated by the company's founder himself.

My proprietor explained the award was given to people who represented Walt Disney's vision, who were passionate cast members and showed up every day with the Disney-loving part of their hearts on fire. Anyone who knew anything at all about me knew how much I enjoyed what I did as part of the pixie dust making machine, and I always carried a healthy amount of Disney history and heritage facts with me, ready to share with anyone who would listen. The award committee proved to be an outstanding opportunity, and I got to work alongside some of those same people for years to come.

My experience on Universal committees was a little different. In one instance, I became part of a committee designed to create an agility program for stunt and action auditions. Several of us worked with the evaluation team to create a program that would provide quick, easy measurements of performance metrics that Universal could use to ensure safety standards were being met. The committee itself was created reactively, after a performer struggled to get out of an emergency situation in a show because they lacked upper body strength. On another committee, we created a program of employee-only offerings.

If you get wind of any committees being assembled, either locally, within the park, or property wide, ask to be considered. In most places, serving on a committee still counts as company business, so you'll be on the clock. Even more importantly, being part of a committee means you are a decision-maker for the future. The things you discuss and the actions you put into play will affect not only those you work with, but the tens of thousands you see every day but will never meet. You could be laying the foundation for generations of people to come, and that's a pretty amazing thing when you think about it.

Teams are in many ways the same as committees, except they are normally not ad hoc. Rather, they are ongoing groups that focus on safety, technology, wardrobe, performance indicator assessments, awards, recognition, and anything else that needs a permanent committee for decision-making or evaluations. Sometimes teams will cycle through different members, giving new people opportunities to get involved, but there are typically the same few members who serve as group chairs and are present at each meeting.

Let's move on to *BETA TESTING*. It's rumored, by those reasonably well-informed, that somewhere in the vaults of Walt Disney enterprises is a secreted away collection of Walt Disney's great, hitherto untouched, ideas. Some of them were apparently transcribed by people he conversed with while alive, and some of them are said to be scribbled out on napkins, stray sheets of notebook paper, or whatever else was handy, in many cases by Walt himself. Imagineering is sitting on these ideas until technology can catch up to the point where executing these visions would be both practical and realized to the degree that Walt envisioned. While I can confidently say Walt Disney is not cryogenically suspended somewhere, it's not at all beyond the realm of possibility such a repository of these notes and sketches in fact exists.

Much of the technology responsible for the smooth sailing of a Disney World guest's day started out as a beta test. In the same way that attractions get soft openings or restaurants have preview nights, beta testing serves as a way to run performance tests on technology in real world scenarios. For this to take place, the company needs volunteers, and during the early research and development phases, these volunteers are typically cast members. I was fortunate enough to be part of two different teams testing Magic Bands before they were released. I've gotten to experience attractions and shows before they were open to the public and share my insights upon exiting, and I've even gotten a first go at menu items for new dining experiences. Even when you hear about invite-only soft opens for these new, paint-not-yet-dried offerings, many of these attractive events have already been test driven by cast members and team members.

While beta tests sound like a great way to a free night's accommodation or a free meal, they're also career opportunities. Your honest assessment of whatever experience you're trying out, delivered to the right people or when prompted at the end of the evaluation, can help inform the operational measurements the company is looking to gauge. As a result, participating in beta tests can get you noticed for all the right reasons. As someone who is safety and detail oriented, I don't focus on the negatives when looking for ways that things could go wrong. I am identifying challenges that could be problematic for the operation itself. These are the kinds of insights I shared the very first time we got to do a Magic Band test. Going into the test, there had already been a number of concerns expressed. Some worried about the people behind the counter not being entirely familiar with technology, leaving them unable to troubleshoot should things go wrong. Some were concerned about what would happen if the device didn't work when someone got to their room, and I questioned whether someone could steal the Magic Band signal the same way RFID frequency data is captured from credit cards or other devices. The first two things were precisely situations that came up during the tests. Granted, the technology was in its infancy, but there were plenty of people behind the counter who had no idea what to do in oddball scenarios, and a few people who had never even seen a Magic Band prior to the first round of testing. During this round, the cast members involved were staying in Coronado Springs. For us, only one of our Magic Bands worked, locking the rest of our party out of our rooms. When we went back to the front desk - a considerable distance away from our rooms in a resort that size - our bands were rescanned, and we were told that would fix the problem. When we got back to the rooms, none of the bands were working.

In fact, our very first experience with the Magic Bands had so many things going wrong that I got the impression the front desk manager was embarrassed, even though none of this was his fault. He was so apologetic, he offered to discount our meal if we were going to dine at the resort. We reassured him that we knew what we were getting into when we signed up for the test and there was no need to feel bad. By the time this conversation took place, we had been to the front desk four times, the last trek done in a golf cart because a cast member working the desk felt awful that we had to hike back and forth (if you've ever stayed at Coronado Springs, you know how capacious the resort is). We were certainly getting our steps in! Even despite these challenges, when asked to give our final feedback about the Magic Bands, we were careful to share our insights intelligently and without belligerence.

If you are going to share a challenge in such situations, share one that is less obvious or personal, but do it all with respect. When you do it that way, people are more inclined to value what you say.

Because of the feedback I provided, I was asked back twice to test the Magic Band technology. I assure you I took full advantage of the staycations provided, but I made sure to remain under the radar and provide plenty of actionable feedback. This is critical. When sharing any challenge that crops up in the test, either observed or personally experienced, always have a solution—even if it doesn't entirely make sense yet. At least when you offer a potential solution, it shows you are approaching the situation with a "yes and" mindset. Even if it's not your job to find the perfect solution, being a participant at ground level means little things that could make these situations run more smoothly might be more apparent to you than to anyone else. If you come up with a good idea, there's a chance it'll be integrated into the fix, and even if you are not officially recognized as the source, somebody, somewhere, has paid attention.

One suggestion I made to the manager was that instead of having to go through the Walt Disney World Resort reservation system phone tree, they have a dedicated phone line at the resort for guests who encounter problems with their Magic Bands. This made immediate assistance readily available for people experiencing difficulties with the new technology. He agreed with me that in today's technology-driven world, immediate service with the human touch always has a place.

At both Disney and Universal, these soft opens and research and development style tests apply to restaurants and park attractions as well. Those involved receive vouchers and time slots to check out new offerings for quick serve or full serve dining locations. The menus themselves are limited, as the focus is more on seeing how everything in the guest experience, from arrival to engagement to departure, worked. For us, it was a free meal and a sneak peek into an offering not yet open to day guests. To those paying attention, it's also an opportunity to observe problem-solving on the fly. When a company does something like this, there's a little more grace at play because they're working with employees, not actual paying guests. Our only responsibility as fill-in customers is to provide feedback when asked. The same thing applies to a new attraction or a show. The dynamics of people on the ride or in the audience change the energy of the experience. It also allows the operations team to identify contingencies and how those should be performed. Soft opens allow challenges to be ferreted out before the larger influx of humanity crush the entrance for the first time.

Then there are *SHADOW OPPORTUNITIES*. If you ever decided you want to know what it's like to be a manager, either in your current line of theme park work or anywhere else, talk to the leader on your team you connect with most. For me, I knew I wanted to be a manager when I started teaching Traditions. A show producer for our stunt show encouraged me to get into leadership years prior, but I just didn't feel like I was ready yet. Things happen when they are supposed to happen, and I never regretted waiting until I felt the siren call and spark for leadership personally.

In these cases, you can be connected with an existing manager and get a feel for a day in the life. Talk to your team leader and get an idea of where you might want to shadow. Shadowing doesn't even have to last a full day, as you can learn a great deal by simply spending a few hours with a manager and talking to people in the operation. This is another great way to get your name and face out there for when managerial positions open up. Even if management is not on your radar, opportunities to shadow an hourly cast member abound. It's a sure-fire way of gaining more knowledge about an operation by working side by side with someone intimately familiar. That was exactly how I got to learn about an element of the children's recreation program. Part of our Traditions training was shadowing an hourly cast member in an operation or line of business different from our own. It is designed to allow us to experience an operation outside of our regular gig. I asked for anything except attraction ops, because I had five years of service in attractions. That day was so much fun and gave me a solid appreciation for the level of trust afforded those at the front lines of this every day. The pay off was playing pirate with a bunch of kids, sailing the not so high seas of the Seven Seas Lagoon. If you are a parent, You can rest easy knowing your kid is not only in good hands, but will come back to shore with new stories, friends and a wonderful core memory.

I've mentioned *CROSS UTILIZATION* (or Cross-U) opportunities before as a great way to both earn additional income and learn about operations other than your own, even if they're ultimately in the same line of business. Depending on your union classification, if you can pick up additional shifts, either within your own department or beyond, I would encourage you to do so. If you're interested in growing with the company, these extra shifts give you the chance to sit in the driver's seat and test drive the vehicle before committing to buying, so to speak. Even within your own department, you shouldn't ignore such opportunities, no matter if you are with Disney or Universal (or any other theme park operation) for the long-haul. Character entertainers, live show performers, and food and beverage cast members, for example, have a host of offerings available to them in terms of special events, separate ticketed events, and holiday events in which they can get involved. A Cross-U is a great way to learn about what positions are out there. You are literally getting paid to learn. Not only do you get an inside peak at how a different branch of the theme park or resort operation is run, but you can experience the culture of that particular location firsthand. If it doesn't feel like a good fit, you never have to go back because you're still safe and secure in your original position. Consider a cross utilization the halfway point between a shadow and a transfer.

Next, let's look at *TRANSFERS*. Suppose you are searching for opportunities beyond your current placement. Maybe you would like to leave attractions operations and go into entertainment. Perhaps you want to leave entertainment and go into food and beverage, or leave food and beverage to become a wrangler at the Tri-Circle D. Maybe you want to be on the opening team of a new attraction, restaurant, show or park. Or you've decided you want to leave the show and be part of show support. Perhaps you have done a marathon's worth of walking in parades and are simply ready for something new. There are processes in place that enable these career shifts. In most cases, they are fairly easy to navigate. There's a pretty clear and specific set of protocols for transferring within your department or out of it. Have a clear picture of where you want to eventually end up and speak with a team manager to get advice on the best way to accomplish the transfer. Great attendance, great attitude, and excellent relationships will help you get there. I mention attendance because it's one of the most important things to pay attention to. Maintaining an exemplary attendance record card is a key component, regardless of how perfect you might be for the role. I also mentioned attitude. Attitude is your fuel for climbing the altitudes within the company. The people with great attitudes are the ones who are prioritized for opportunities, invited to participate in new experiences and get on the schedule for one-on-ones. This isn't the most apt comparison, but it's relatively like schoolyard play. Those who play well with others tend to play more than those who bully others on the playground. This is a life hack. Playing well with others gets you further in life. Nobody accomplishes anything on their own.

The first thing that happens when you apply for a transfer is a record card review. If you exceed the number of absences permitted by transfer guidelines, you won't be able to transfer, even if you're the most amazing cast member or team member in the history of the Walt Disney Company or Universal. If you don't yet qualify for a transfer because of attendance (or other reasons), asking for feedback is a great way to demonstrate continued interest. Sometimes people get squirrelly with the word "feedback", but no other resource has been as valuable to me in the professional world. Even as an Equity performer, all the feedback in the world was available to me, but I had to ask for it. According to our union agreement, there were some stipulations on what the company could or couldn't share with me, but if I ever openly asked my stage managers for feedback, they provided it freely. Even at Universal, your peers working the roles you want and the managers you have great relationships with are the ones who will be your most ardent advocates. With every live show I have ever done, I always found myself in a position where I was trying to figure the best way to accomplish a stunt, hit a note or sell an action. While there might be competition at contract time, that won't stop most from providing guidance. Veteran performers are a wonderful resource as you learn and grow.

Feedback in the workplace is similar to rehearsal notes; it gives us a chance to improve and realign focus. When you ask for feedback, request it from a manager or show director you have a good rapport with, preferably someone who has worked with you. These people can provide an honest and unflinching appraisal of where you excel and what you can improve on. You should listen! After all, these are the people who have had firsthand experience at observing and working with you. All feedback is a gift, even if you may not agree with it or find yourself being sensitive to it.

Another excellent reason to ask for feedback is that the person providing it likely has experience in your line of business. Asking them to weigh in with their own perspectives is an excellent way to bolster your own knowledge, so don't ever react to feedback defensively. It's nothing less than a chance to grow.

As for attitude? You can have the best attendance record in the history of any park where you've punched a timecard, but if your attitude makes you the bane of everyone's existence the moment you appear, you're not going to get the transfer you want. As you go through the process, it's highly probably someone will reach out to one of your managers. What this manager has to say about your performance - backstage or onstage - is going to determine how far you get through the transfer and interview process. This isn't the standard employment confirmation call a potential outside employer makes before hiring you, where someone reaches out to Universal, Disney or whatever park you worked at to confirm you did work there (these companies will typically provide length-of-time service dates for such calls). Within the companies themselves, when you're looking to move from one line of business to another, or even move within the same operation (think food and beverage quick serve to The California Grill, or entertainment characters to Equity or live shows), anything and everything is on the table. You can trust your manager will talk about you with great candor. This is why cultivating good relationships is so important. If you cannot qualify for a transfer because you haven't been in a position long enough, focus on doing everything you can to rise above the fray. Even while performing as part of a team, you can still allow your individual efforts to shine.

Be aware of this during your quest for your next wonderful opportunity: a job title is rarely as simple as stated, and never all-encompassing. The same title can function differently depending on the park or location. For example, Disney Photo Imaging (DPI) can be managed in a variety of ways, and the daily performance expectations can vary depending on where you're based. Taking photos on Sunset Boulevard at Disney's Hollywood Studios, versus taking pictures at Typhoon Lagoon or Disney Springs, versus capturing a little real-world magic photographing an engagement, are just a few places where the same job title is met with drastically different day-to-day expectations. At Disney, in the gated parks (that is, a park where you pay an entrance fee to enter), such positions are typically part of a rotation. Roving positions are put into play when staffing allowances permit. At the gated water parks your position can include shooting characters then moving to take shots of families with icons. From there you might spend some time roving, all as part of the same shift.

With the DPI operation, you can be tapped to shoot sporting events at the Sports Complex for Game Day photos or assigned to shoot a particular field, court, team, or player. Photo Imaging also includes the Disney Entertainment Group (DEG), so you could be deployed to a shipboard position as a DCL ship photographer. DPI alone offers a vast number of options, just within the Disney photography operation. There's equipment support, inventory, and many other parts of the operation that require staffing. At Universal, attractions rotations and support positions operate more or less in the same fashion. The bottom line here is that a line of business is more than the business itself: it is the people, with their various backgrounds and responsibilities, who make the operation work in the first place.

At both Universal and Disney, your versatility and skills can make you highly sought after. I've worked with people in entertainment at both companies who demonstrated an incredible ability to learn choreography, lines, music, or media interactions. In some cases, these actors had their own following of day guests and annual pass-holders, always on the lookout to see where their favorite performers had landed and making these performers generally sought after by stage productions. There are people at Disney and Universal who have performed on just about every stage that has ever existed at the parks. These individuals have had contracts for decades; they have been the face of iconic characters for everything from Disney's "Hoop Dee Doo Revue" to Halloween Horror Nights to the Universal Macy's Thanksgiving Day Parade.

A friend's daughter, Annie, who started in a merchandising role at the World of Disney at Disney Springs, went into the company unsure of what her next steps should be. She spent a year at that location and wanted to branch out. We had a conversation, and I told her a great way to see what else was out there, while still getting paid, was to pick up extra hours. Even though operations does a wonderful job at predicting their staffing needs, day-to-day operations can be fluid depending on attendance and callouts. Large venues like the Fantasmic Theater at Disney's Hollywood Studios can always use extra staffing. You're going to have a better chance at a transfer if you've demonstrated previous association with that line of business, even if you're working in something as straightforward as crowd control. Annie wound up traveling from merchandising to food and beverage, on to attractions operations then back to merchandising, and finally landed in attractions operations for the Slinky Dog Dash, a role she'd been eyeing since the beginning. Indeed, it became a perfect fit for her.

At Universal, the same mantra applies: the more you know, the further you go. Picking up hours at various attractions gives you a better idea of the protocols and standard operating procedures for each one. This is beneficial in so many ways. I know plenty of people who wind up working long but enjoyable days because they move on from their main shift to pick up hours in another location. This is not only rewarding in a financial sense, but they're also getting their names out there as reliable employees. I did this all the time when I was an attractions host at Disney. There were plenty of shifts where I worked from opening to closing and did so gladly. The operation had the budget, and my presence provided guaranteed staffing.

One of my DPI coordinators, Blake, knew the Disney Photo Imaging coordinator operation for every park because he picked up extra shifts all the time. He was in such high demand that once, at the end of his shift, the closing manager from another park offered to both give him drive-on access (convenient because it would also cut fifteen minutes off his walk to the operation center) and buy him dinner. Even though Blake would have taken the shift regardless, it's always nice to be recognized and rewarded. If you ever find yourself in a managerial role, make sure to recognize and thank individuals on your team when they go above and beyond.

There's another reason why it's important to make yourself aware of every option out there. The one rock you don't turn over could be the very one holding the key to the next door. Learn everything you can; even if you only get to observe the operation as a guest, your cast member/team member filter will help you notice things other won't. Learning about an operation in person helps you understand the ways in which a job description posted on a website isn't comprehensive, at least not comprehensive enough to give you a complete picture of the world into which you'd be stepping. Being physically present gives you the opportunity to talk to managers, cast members and team members, including people who have just transferred. Try to ask questions beyond, "What do you think of working here?" Treat every managerial meet-and-greet like a conversational interview. Just like any interview, be prepared to explain why you want to work in a particular role, attraction, or location, and expect to be prompted to ask your own questions at the end. I always ask these two: "If you could change one thing about your organization, what would it be?" After the answer, I follow up with, "What is the one thing about this operation that gets you up in the morning, excited to be a part of the day?" I am not trying to be clever - I simply want to know what the people at the helm think of the ship. When one of the interviewers turned the question back on me, I answered, "I'm not a part of this operation yet, so it's hard for me to say. But it looks like people are having a lot of fun, and that's a place I'd like to be."

The questions may seem subjective, but in an interview, both parties are exploring whether they would be a good fit for each other. It is the business equivalent of speed dating. There's nothing wrong with asking such questions, and you should always try to dig a little deeper into someone's personal experience to learn more about a position. One additional thing you ought to pay attention to is the environment. Not just the people, but the space. Are the positions outside? Are there smells or other issues? What does the break space look like? Are the managers accessible to their team? It is similar to when one is house shopping. The neighborhood might look great during the day, but what happens nights and weekends? Does the landfill down the street provide a wafting perfume you'd rather not have to enjoy? For every element of polished onstage presentation, there are backstage areas that have been neglected. That can impact morale, performance, and the desire to even show up.

Here's another thing to keep in mind: you can always say "no" when approached about a transfer. If it's not the right time for you, be gracious but honest. Accepting a job that you don't feel is a great fit for can lead to frustration, burnout, or enmity with the area or company. If you can support yourself on a part-time position, taking such a position in a department until you're certain enough of the fit can often be a better choice, career wise, than taking a full-time role in a place you're not excited about. Remember, you can always pick up shifts park-wide to make up the extra hours.

It's also perfectly acceptable to turn down an offer. In my experience, at both Disney and Universal, there's no such thing as a "one and done" chance. I'm not suggesting that this is always the case, but for me, I was never given an ultimatum when it came to opportunities. I was approached about going into Disney management several years before I made the decision to pursue a managerial position on my own. I wasn't trying to be stubborn about it, and I have nothing but respect and affection for the leader who tried to guide me into management all those years ago. The simple truth of the matter was that it just wasn't the right time for me.

TEMPORARY ASSIGNMENTS (TAs) are another great way to discover opportunities out of your normal or regular wheelhouse, and they're exactly what they sound like. No matter the specifics of the post, temporary assignments are always a benefit for your career. If you hear about a TA position that sounds like something you'd be interested in, learn everything you can about the responsibilities of the role. If there are information sessions, attend one (in most cases, attendance at an information session is mandatory to be considered for the role, whether it is hourly or salaried). You are not cheating by doing research and preparation. Quite the opposite. Such efforts demonstrate your initiative.

TA positions can be part of a rollout team, or they can be temporary assignments that constantly rotate with staffing adjustments every six, nine, or twelve months. No matter what, there are two main things to consider. Number one: a temporary assignment can be just that, temporary. If you land the role and discover it's not exactly something you want to do, dig your heels in and do the very best you can. When the role ends, you get to go back to your previous location, but you leave behind a performance that will be evaluated. This is good. Why? There is a strong chance the leader or hiring manager of an area you've had your eye will hear about your OTJ (on the job) performance. In the same way a member of an audition team might consider you for a role you were not auditioning for, a similar thing happens in these cases (this is exactly how I landed my first TA, which lasted eighteen months). Number two: if this temporary assignment turns out to be precisely the sort of thing you would like to do, you guessed it - dig your heels in and do the very best you can. Knock your managers and their managers off their feet with your performance, and don't be surprised if they offer to extend your TA or transfer you into their operation to status you there permanently.

If a TA position gives you the chance to be a salaried leader, only take it if it's something you're interested in. You don't have to love it, and it doesn't have to be the starting point to your dream career, but if you feel like you don't fit in with the operational and cultural dynamics for a particular line of business, it will be a constant struggle. This could even work against you in the long run. If you decide to take the gig, inquire as to whether there's any kind of attached leadership training (at Disney, this would be the Emerging Leaders

Program). Almost every salaried park and resort leadership position starts out as a TA, with executive positions as the sometimes-typical exception (I say sometimes because plenty of executives at both Universal and Disney started their careers as hourly team or cast members). Do not be quick to judge if your background is food and beverage or entertainment and you are given a custodial manager TA opportunity. The operational responsibilities may differ, but at the end of the day you are there to support your team. Take care of your people, and they'll take care of the operation. When that happens, everyone looks like a rock star.

Temporary assignments give all parties a chance to see if they fit together. At Disney, I've known plenty of hourly cast members who returned to their original operation once their TA concluded, either because they preferred that location, or they simply weren't ready to take on the permanent responsibilities associated with the role, something many easily relate to. Others used the experience to guide them towards still new opportunities. Some found themselves starting a TA and eyeing the exit within the first week, only to discover by the end of the assignment they had become fond of the operation and its people. With TAs, keep an open mind. With TAs, do what works for *you*. Every TA role I've joined had an adequate starting point for new hires. Whenever I took on a TA role, I was a careful note-taker. It was important for me to take time and break down the basic expectations and responsibilities for each role, and I ended up keeping these notes as a source document that could be modified to reflect current performance standards. This allowed me to identify needs and redundancies in each role and leave behind a guide that others new to an operation or line of business could follow. The genesis for this idea came from my first TA. The operation I had been brought into hadn't had a TA onboarded in over six years. Protocols, resources, and contacts had all changed dramatically on the one-sheet (a literal sheet with a checklist of individuals and departments to contact with questions) that they gave me. Creating such reference materials is a way of not only helping yourself, but helping the operation and leaving a legacy. When you build bridges, others take notice as they walk across.

If you are considering a TA, ask your leadership team (or any leader you have a good rapport with, even a captain, coordinator, or team leader) to do a mock interview with you. This helps work out your nerves and bugs, and it allows you to create ready-to-go pocket pitches for the standard interview questions. If you are asked about how you managed conflict in the workplace, a guest disappointment, or any other sort of challenge, having a quick and honest response will show you've already considered what it takes to work in such a public facing job. Using real-life examples are a plus. In most cases, the managers working you through your mock interviews have hosted the real things before, and they can talk you through performance tips and what to expect. Remember, if your manager is helping you, it's because they believe in you for the role. Show your appreciation for any leader who takes the time to help you; they have added assisting you in your career pursuits to an already-full schedule.

Moving from position to position is perceived differently at Disney and Universal than in the rest of the employment world. In the theme park and resort entertainment world, being transferred from one line of business to another, or even within the LoB itself, is what makes you a better, more educated, and well-rounded leader. There's no such thing in the corporate entertainment world as a "serial transferrer". If or when you decide to leave the world of theme park magic-making, it is important to understand you will have to explain this, just in case you're ever asked why you "didn't seem capable of holding onto a job for longer than six to twelve months". For you and your theme park journey, every new experience you gain only adds to your value and knowledge base. There were plenty of learning moments for me where experience in one operation helped me to understand why things at another were done a certain way.

There are also some resort, park, and operational specifics I'd like to touch on, the first of which is the *DISNEY CRUISE LINE*. If you're headed onto a Disney ship, think both about the role you're stepping into and where you want to end up. DCL is in some ways similar to working at a park, and in other ways like working at a resort. You will have the opportunity to wear several hats. As a leader, if staffing challenges arise, you could find yourself as a senior entertainment officer and an Assistant Cruise Director simultaneously. On many cruise ships, being hired into entry level or baseline "Entertainment" means being a dancer in a show, a character performer at a meet-and-greet, and an assistant at bingo. All in one day. Just as in the parks, working several roles give you the chance to learn and demonstrate your proficiency and ability. Shine and show off those abilities every single time you get the chance. As I've mentioned before, it doesn't matter where you are, people are always watching. On a cruise ship, the optics are magnified. DCL tends to have a higher crew member-to-guest ratio than other cruise lines in the industry, which means a greater likelihood of visibility and advancement. Disney is also a huge proponent of promoting from within, which can include moving people from the parks to the ships, and vice versa, so your performance on deck can directly affect the opportunities awaiting you when your feet touch dry land again.

BRAND AWARENESS TOURS also bear mentioning, whether taking them or giving them. These are great opportunities to learn about how a specific attraction or show operates. As a creator or tour provider, you get to become an expert on the stage you're promoting. You'll learn all the great trivia about the location, along with its history and the specifics of how it's run. Tours are a great way to feel out whether working at the operation would be of any long-term interest for you. At Disney, sign-ups for a brand awareness tour take place either through Disney University, or at the location itself. With theme parks, as a rule, you can find people passionate about their attractions who lean into learning and share that enthusiasm with anyone who is interested. At Universal, many times you can just approach someone who works at a given show, position, or attraction. They are like living easter eggs! At both parks I had the good fortune of meeting front line team and cast members who were happy to dive into the trivia and day-in-the-job-life of attractions like Hogwarts, The American Adventure, Men in Black, Pandora, and The Haunted Mansion. If there is a show, attraction, or even themed restaurant with wide-spread appeal, there is likely trivia and a tour associated with the space or place.

Lastly, look into becoming a *VOLUNTEER* or *VOLUNTEER COORDINATOR*. Universal has a host of programs designed to support the local community. Through the Resort Community Relations team, Universal deploys team members who volunteer for youth programs and The Universal Foundation. They also work closely with the Make a Wish Foundation, The Boys and Girls Club of Central Florida, A Gift for Teaching, Habitat for Humanity, and Junior Achievement (JA), just to name a few.

When I first started with Universal, we did a short program for JA, designed to highlight the partnership of Universal with the organization. It took place at the Cheyenne Saloon, part of the Church Street complex in downtown Orlando. A few 'troublemakers' showed up, got loud and caused a good old-fashioned bar brawl. Afterward, we were peppered with questions, which gave us the opportunity to further educate. It was great fun for everyone involved and really emphasized the commitment Universal had to the organization. Anytime you see a massive group of people deployed in purple shirts, there's a good chance they are Universal volunteers.

Disney also has a volunteer network of cast members, called VoluntEars. Just like with Universal, these cast members spend hundreds of thousands of hours volunteering every single year, frequently through a coordinated effort between Disney's volunteer program and the organizations who need volunteers. Everything from animal rescue to Give Kids the World to Habitat for Humanity. As a cast member, if you want to volunteer but aren't sure where or how, there are plenty of contact points. Taking it a step further, becoming a volunteer coordinator for your local area is an excellent way to generate interest in volunteering among your fellow cast and team members.

Maybe you're working in an area that needs a point person for Toys for Tots. Maybe you're a parent with a vested interest in a back-to-school campaign, or perhaps you remember with fondness being a recipient of a backpack replete with school supplies and want to give back to an organization that supported you all those years ago. These opportunities and more are there for the taking.

Tips and Tricks for Excelling as a Theme Park Employee

<u>ENGAGE IN TEAM BUILDING</u>.

I have been very fortunate during my time in the theme park universe, no matter whether it was live shows or attractions operations. In attractions, I was part of a group that would go out together, on average, once a week. Usually, we went to EPCOT and walked around

World Showcase. Our goal wasn't to grab drinks or a meal, though that would happen. These outings were just a chance for us to hang out together outside of work. Years later, I experienced something similar. Training under cloak and dagger circumstances in the Wonders Lot, prior to the grand opening of our stunt show "Lights Motors Action" (LMA), was both exciting and filled with tremendous pressure. Many of us were learning and practicing stunts we'd never done before, things like jumping cars, and driving on two wheels. Learning and doing these stunts without banging up the car or one's body was a real exercise in discipline (you haven't lived until you get bit by your steering wheel while throwing back-to-back 180s). Going to Epcot as a team was a great way to blow off steam at the end of the day. At Universal, both when I was at "T2" and "The Wild, Wild Wild West Stunt Show", we often would get together off property to socialize.

There are plenty of options, both formal and casual, official and unofficial, when it comes to team building with your theme park coworkers. The Walt Disney World resort has its own recreational area for cast members, Little Lake Bryan. They will occasionally open this space up for family-oriented events, though it's typically an employee-only area. This location is nice because of its variety of recreational opportunities, pavilions, and open spaces. Your team builder can be something as simple as a pop-up softball game. During my time at the company, I frequented Mickey's Retreat on a regular basis. Typically, those who know about the place use it, and those who don't know are surprised when they find out it exists (and wish they had learned about it sooner). It's a beautiful, bucolic location in the middle of the hustle and bustle of housing and commerce. As a cast member, it is a perk there just for you.

At Disney and Universal, team builders can and do take place at the resorts. Fishing, bowling, and, of course, brand awareness, are just a few of the many things that await at both park and resort operations.

Once the LMA stage opened, our team building activities diversified. One activity favorite was the fishing excursions with the Recreation team and fishing guides based the Contemporary Resort. We'd meet at 5:30 a.m., fish for a few hours, and get to the stage well in advance for our day's performances. Managers, techs, actors, attraction hosts, and stunt drivers? There was no caste system. Everyone was welcome.

At Universal, my team would frequently go to movies, a local restaurant, or golfing. At "Terminator", a video console often was set up after training. We'd watch Halo being played on those massive screens. Managers brought in pizza, and we all hung out together. There were flag football games between stages, trivia competitions between venues, and the occasional cast member paintball game. Even in attraction operations, team builders can be as simple as a game of rock-paper-scissors to determine who does the first show or checks out the ride vehicles. At "The Great Movie Ride," there was a version of roulette played to determine the performer for the first show. All the Cowboys who would grab their single actions and go into the heart of the attraction. With a single blank in each one, you'd spin the cylinders and then safely fire, with weapons pointed up. If your weapon dry-fired, you were safe. If you detonated your blank, you had first show. At LMA, besides the official team builders, one activity brought everyone together. If someone was leaving the stage either because they were transferring into another operation or they were leaving the company, their going away celebration included being launched into the canal that was a part of our stage. The person leaving never knew when it was going to happen. The only reason it never happened to me what is because I was offered to leadership position on a Thursday and I started that position on a Sunday. I left my stage and did not return for another 19 months, and only then to reset my clock, which was a technicality for anyone placed into a TA. I was OK not being thrown into the canal (At least that water wasn't as frightening as the Lagoon at Universal Studios. If anyone fell into that water during a show, they were immediately transported to health services… to get a tetanus shot.)

Teamwork makes the dream work. It's more than just a delivery of a product that guarantees positive reactions and outcomes. Sometimes, it's simply a matter of being in the trenches, of understanding what is necessary so that you can provide the best product possible. Many times, the people on these teams are the ones who celebrate your wins and help you overcome your challenges. It is very much the same as the sense a family that develops from working on the stage sure as part of a touring production. The teams that work at these attractions build long-term relationships and team builders are one part of that. It happens for a variety of reasons, but the outcome is the same: you build better relationships because you get to know people.

During my time serving as a member of the 40th anniversary Traditions team, we created a brand awareness rotation. Every month, a member of the team would arrange for a brand awareness team builder. One of my fellow Traditions facilitators worked at the haunted mansion, so we got a very special tour of the "Haunted Mansion" before it opened for day guests. Another made arrangements for us to ride spaceship first and then tour the attraction after it's operational day had completed. We got to experience Soarin, "Kilimanjaro Safari", and "Pandora" in this fashion. For my part, I brought the entire team in to experience the content I had created for Disney University. They watched the warm-up, they watched the show and then they got a tour of the stage afterward. I brought out the remote car so everybody had a chance to sit in the carriage attached to the side of the Hero car and get an idea for what that felt like.

When you have a blast working with friends nothing feels like work.

<u>BECOME A SUBJECT MATTER EXPERT</u>.

I was passionate and knowledgeable about the history of the Walt Disney Company, and that meant people learned to come to me with questions. Those who knew I also worked at Universal would hit me up with the same queries. The questions range from trivia-driven to practical. When there were special ticketed events, like Halloween Horror Nights, or Mickey's Not-So-Scary Halloween Party, they wanted insider know-how. If they had family coming into town, or they were bringing people to one of the parks, they wanted to share information and be in-the-know. A secondary aspect of this information accumulation and dissemination involved the knowledge I developed creating the tour for the "Lights Motors Action" stage. I got questions ranging from, "How do we keep the stage safe?" to "Where did you conduct your research?" I'm a huge fan of vetting information sources. If I had to attribute credit, I'd suggest the mindset came from my first leader and his belief that we should always *trust but verify*.

The safety piece for LMA was easy. I researched OSHA recordables and spoke to the people in charge of global safety at the Walt Disney World resort. I brought my own experience with stunt shows and film and TV stunt work into the conversation. Creating the tour was simply a matter of speaking to Imagineers, doing additional research, and having the incredible fortune of talking to people involved with building and training the original "Moteurs, Action!" car stunt show in Paris. It was easy for me to take in all the information because I love learning. That's part of the reason why visiting Disney to see the beautiful buildings and experience the attractions wasn't enough for me. I had to know the whys and hows behind it all. Turns out, knowing the why made me a better cast member. It will make you a better employee at any park or resort as well.

Part of what makes the magic of Disney so special for guests is getting to unravel its execution. I once participated in a Universal tour of Hogwarts, where I learned that a vast number of the props and set pieces found decorating the attraction's queue were straight from the films and their myriad sets. Learning behind-the-scenes details about how these operations run makes the experience no less magical, and even when park guests have no idea, they can still feel the authenticity of each detail.

BE OPEN, AGILE AND RESPONSIVE.

Disney taught me the importance of thinking "blue sky" and being able to quickly connect the dots and respond to challenges. Blue sky initiatives typically resemble think-tanks and are rarely the result of one individual. You get people together and spitball ideas, seeing what sticks and seeing how the ideas connect. It's important not to be afraid, take risks and fail on the journey to making discoveries, growing as a result. Thankfully, I had a great deal of experience with the failing part as an actor, author, and stuntman. I'm not saying I was a failure. To the contrary, I've continued to enjoy a wonderful, robust career in entertainment. It's simply that these kind of things will get you told "no, thank you" way more than "yes". None of the above are considered jobs in the conventional sense. They don't guarantee you get to show up to work every day, collect a paycheck, and go home. You have to constantly put yourself way out there, market yourself, and self-manage. You must make sure you're always putting yourself out there. So much goes into this process. For me, risk-taking isn't nearly as frightening as shrugging off an opportunity.

Disney also taught me a great deal about agility and responsiveness. I learned the earliest of these lessons in context as a guest at both Disney and Universal. I'd leave the park one day, and when I came back the next, I'd see holiday décor, garlands, and trees everywhere. Overnight, these parks were magically transformed. I keep calling it magical, but there's truly no other word for it. Whether you are working at Disney or Universal, there's a *je ne sais quoi* that touches your soul when you walk up the street that a scarce twenty-four hours prior had been its everyday self, only to see it liveried in its finest holiday sparkle. These were magical goosebump moments for me… even for someone who worked there for years.

Speaking to agility, when *Frozen* came out, Disney appeared not to have expected the response it got (my observation and not the official company line). The public response was earth shattering. In a month's time, it seemed like the entire world was singing "Let It Go". The Orlando resort operation responded. In a few weeks, an entire "Frozen Summer Fun" project launched. There were meet and greets, food displays, specialty fireworks, viewing parties, and merchandise options. What really blew me away? In less than one month's time, Disney's creative team of Imagineers had transformed one of the sound stages into an entire Frozen Winter Wonderland. From concept to inception, magic happened. There was an outpost, a meet and greet with characters from the movie, and a place where you could play in the snow - real, actual snow. They built a skating rink inside the sound stage where some truly incredible performances were put on the ice. When performances weren't happening, you could rent skates and go ice skating. If skating wasn't your thing, you could get big cups of hot chocolate with marshmallows floating on top, accompanied by delicious gingerbread cookies, and sit there bundled up, enjoying the view. They did a not surprisingly brisk business of moving sweatshirts off of the shelves. In the central Florida summer, the soundstage was that chilly.

If a global entertainment giant like Disney could respond with such agility, imagine what you can do when you get wind of an opportunity for the taking. Disney taught me not to be afraid to reach for the door when opportunity knocks. The worst thing that can happen is you get told no. You might discover it's not exactly what you want to buy or buy into, or you don't quite achieve what you were aiming to. It's always a learning opportunity. You don't get exposure without putting yourself out there in the first place. Remember, you miss all the chances you don't take.

CREATE OPPORTUNITIES.

Throughout your journey, seeking insight and advice from others is critical, and it can often lead to self-created opportunities. In other words, feedback is a gift. In fact, a great example of this was my journey to teach Traditions. The year prior to "my year", I showed up to Disney University, hoping to learn how to get myself in front of a Traditions classroom, the Golden Grail of Disney Knowledge. To be honest, I had no idea what went into the process; I just knew I had to do it. I ran into Anthony in the hallway outside the Traditions leadership offices, and I told him why I was there. As it happened, I had missed the last information session of the year and there was nothing he could do. He wrote his email address on the back of an envelope and gave it to me, asking me to stay in touch during the year. He said he hoped he'd see me next year, and you know what? I believed him. There was an unmistakable sincerity in his voice.

I stayed in touch and immediately learned from our correspondence that I wasn't even qualified to teach Traditions because I was part of an Equity stage. The Equity collective bargaining agreement prohibited such a position being filled by an AEA performer, even though no one was sure why. I began to pick Anthony's brain, and I also consulted my manager's manager, the proprietor of our area, Lloyd. Both were encouraging well beyond the scope of their roles. Both gave me feedback and advice without which I never would have accomplished my Traditions dream. After speaking to Lloyd and Anthony, I reached out to the local Actors' Equity office and spoke to one of my union representatives, Brian. He was initially resistant to the idea, concerned it was a company initiative, until I explained why teaching Traditions was so important to me. He was right to feel that way, because a good union puts their members first. I told him it was something I felt compelled to do because I remembered how formative the experience had been for me. It was magic, and so impactful that to this day I continue to stay in touch with the two Traditions facilitators from my orientation day.

I told Brian it was all my idea, and I wanted to work with Equity to make it happen. I had learned enough about the Traditions facilitator role by then to speak intelligently about how an Equity cast member could both perform the role and not violate the union's collective bargaining agreement. It would provide additional opportunities for career growth, not just for me, but anyone who wanted to follow in my footsteps. He liked the idea that I was laying the groundwork for others, and that this effort wasn't purely a selfish one (although, to be fair, I was definitely thinking about how to get myself a Traditions audition). Brian was fully on board with the idea and began work on his end to make it happen. I stayed in touch with Anthony and Brian throughout the process and always kept Anthony in the loop, as I also did with Lloyd. I knew everyone directly and indirectly involved supported my efforts, and I wanted to show them how doggedly determined I was to get in front of that Traditions class.

Fast forward to nearly a year later (because good things take time) and Equity, working with Disney, had come up with a solution. That solution happened mere weeks before the first info session. The role was going to be classified as a "Clinician" part (I didn't care what they called it as long as I could audition for Traditions), providing assistance and training to new cast members with strict stipulations on expectations for the role. I was delighted and reached out to thank Brian. I then emailed Anthony to share the good news. He asked if I knew when the information sessions were being held that year, and I told him "I have been following the posting announcements *very* closely this time."

I showed up at the information session, got assigned my topic, and went to work.

In Traditions, no two audition years are the same, but I did learn that the audition process typically starts with a topic. The reason for this? Topics give the Traditions leadership team a chance to see if the auditionees have presence, command of an audience, and can deliver on a topic within a specific timeframe. Traditions is a very tightly run program, and time management is a key component to its success (come to think about it, this is a general hack for life itself). My topic had to appear top-of-the-head extemporizing, even as it would be polished and well-rehearsed.

The topic I was given? *What do I do when I need to refill my pixie dust?*

I knew it would be a fun thing to talk about. I loved Disney so much that I had an annual pass when I studied at Florida Atlantic University and was living in South Florida. I'd get away for the weekend, bring my books, find a bench at World Showcase in EPCOT, and study. When I needed a break, I'd snag something to eat from a quick serve, or treat myself to a full-service, sit-down meal. Honestly, the environment was much better than any study hall, kitchen table, or debatably clean dorm room. Some weekends, when I would spend most of a study day in the UK, Morocco, or Canada, it felt very much like a study abroad program.

During my first audition for Traditions, I told the story of walking into the Magic Kingdom for the very first time. I described it like the beginning of a book, how the magic hit me, and I knew right then and there I had to be a part of this world. Then I talked about being a stunt driver at "Lights Motors Action". I told everyone in the room that when I needed a shot of the good stuff I'd go to, "One Man's Dream" at Disney's Hollywood Studios. Getting to hear Walt Disney himself talk about why Disneyland was built, and why building it was so important to him, felt like getting guidance from the man who knew best - a personalized pep talk from Uncle Walt. If I walked in with a grimace, I always walked out with a grin.

I ended my topic by handing out little 2x3 inch plexiglass cards. Inside was a bunch of glitter, liberally sprinkled, under the message, "In case of Pixie Dust emergency, break glass." Everyone in the room - the auditors from the Traditions team and every other person auditioning - got one. Was I doing the same thing as I did whenever I went in for film, television, and theatrical auditions, where I brought a bag of chocolate or Skittles to hand out? No. In those cases, while I wanted them to remember me, I also knew the people in that room were stuck for hours at a time, and a little snack might be nice. In the case of my Traditions audition, I needed everyone in the room to understand how much I believed in the power of pixie dust, and I wanted to leave everyone keenly aware that for me, the magic was real. For them, it could be, too. They only had to believe.

The multitiered audition process for Traditions was one of the most demanding auditions I ever participated in by that point in my entertainment life. Callback upon callback upon callback.

Because it's different every year, it's harder to give explicit guidance. I can tell you what to do (be yourself, be a source of joy, share your passions, and smile) but not what to expect. When the reveal happened, who other than Lloyd was there to congratulate me with a balloon, Mickey ears, a disposable camera, and a great big hug. Our Traditions team was and is special (we still keep in touch). As we were often reminded, even if it makes no sense, "The year picks you."

Even some among the Traditions leadership team at Disney University remarked on how the year had picked the group of us who were closer and tighter than any Traditions team before since. To this day, any time we get together and we try to do a get together once a year, the first five or so minutes is hugs and tears. That is relationship building at an elevated level.

I became the first Equity cast member to teach Traditions in many, many years, but my determination pioneered the way for others to follow. I didn't care about the bragging rights; I simply wanted to make a difference and saw a personally relevant way in which I could. Now and going forward, people that I'll never even meet get to take part teaching this storied program.

That's a thing you can do in any role or position, no matter the park. Look for a way to make a difference. In my case, at Disney University, I was able to do something permanent that would benefit thousands of cast members to come. Don't ever discount the power that one voice - your voice - can have. Your persistent commitment makes the difference. When you believe, eventually your conviction has others believing, too. In my entire Disney career, teaching Traditions was one of the most incredible Cross-U opportunities I ever experienced, a transformative period that became a brilliant highlight in my time at Disney.

Don't be afraid to create your own opportunities. Remember that trail blazers don't get to where they are going by taking the path already established.

I got to know several cast members who essentially crafted or augmented a secondary role into their jobs. Brian, an hourly cast member who still works as a technician at the Walk Disney World Resort, told me how frustrated he got by the amount of waste generated at his stage. Undertaking his own research, he began building networks within the Walt Disney World Resort in Orlando to recycle everything from food waste to bubble wrap. He found a location on property that would take various kinds of metal, including pot metal. He located a place for old, damaged, or broken electronics. He got his proprietor to approve the purchase of specialty branded hot/cold mugs for every single person associated with his stage. Even if you were a seasonal cast member (CT), you still got one of these colorful cups to hang up in the kitchen, customized with your name. He demonstrated that these mugs would drastically reduce the volume of single-use cups being thrown away. Brian spearheaded such an attack on waste produced that, when he was done, his venue - a massive stage with dozens of cast members and crew - produced less waste per day than could fill a one-gallon trash bag. Brian continues to be very much in demand across the property, with other lines of business seeking his expertise on waste management. He's still a technician, but across all fields of park work, Brian is valued as one of the go-to experts in Disney's property-wide Environmentality initiative. While he wasn't the first innovator of the environmental mindset Disney promotes, he got recognized for the work he did (a labor of love he took on in addition to his daily responsibilities) and became the recipient of a very special name tag. As special as the Legacy name tag is, the tag that Brian received, the one that goes to cast members who bring Environmentality to the forefront of their careers, is even rarer and, in my opinion, equally (if not more) special. This name tag is made from bamboo, a highly sustainable material and versatile in its uses (do the research and you'll find bamboo is used for everything from building materials to clothing). If you see a cast member wearing a bamboo name tag, thank them for making the park, resort operation, and the world a better, more sustainable place.

Then there's Gage, an Entertainment Manager who became concerned about the shortage and relevance of safety documentation and checklists at the stage where he was based, so he began to create his own documents. How important is a checklist? An example many of us can relate to is aviation. Pilots use them before they get into the plane, even before they arrive at the airport. For Gage, it started with the safety basics - literally where the first aid kits were located. Just as cast members in greeter positions should know where to direct guests towards food or bathrooms, Gage felt that people in backstage areas needed to know where to go and what to do in case of a minor or major safety issue. Every time he arrived at a new entertainment venue, making these checklists was the first thing he'd start to work on. He focused on simple information, designed to optimize someone's ability to respond in the event of an emergency. KISS: Keep It Simple, Silly. Gage made a habit of walking an area to identify where the automatic external defibrillators were located. He made sure everyone knew where to find phones and first aid kits, then would ask if people knew the emergency evacuation procedures. He arranged for the Reedy Creek Fire Department to visit and demonstrate how a defibrillator worked and why people shouldn't be afraid to use one. Eventually, he created a checklist and would meet with his stage to lead a Socratic method-style discussion, asking questions and more questions about where these resources were located. If someone stumbled on the answer, Gage would physically lead them to the first aid kit or resource they hadn't been able to mentally or orally place. When he was done, Gage would give everyone a comprehensive review of emergency material locations and protocols. Did people know what to do when a guest needed a Band-Aid, what happens in case of injury, or if someone suffered from heat exhaustion, and when to call 911 for medical attention? When he was finished in an area or operation, everyone knew the safety and response components.

All of this he did in addition to his responsibilities as an entertainment manager. In time, he became Disney's first global entertainment safety manager, visiting different entertainment venues across the property and ensuring everyone was on top of the local, operational safety expectations. When Gage was offered the safety manager position as a full-time role, he never changed his approach. His goal was always to make learning fun for the cast members. His role, when you think about it, is critical to the park's undercurrent of smooth sailing.

At Disney, Safety is the first Key, something every new cast member learns about at Traditions. No guest comes home from a Disney vacation to enthusiastically share that, "Oh boy, Disney was sooooo safe!" Disney cast members think about safety so guests never have to. Gage worked tirelessly to help cast members embrace that cultural safety mindset.

I identified a similar opportunity when I built the tour operation for the "Lights Motors Action" stage. While there was a bit of joking about me creating a position that didn't exist before, the position of "Tour Manager", it became an invaluable offer for both Disney University and the Disney Institute. People wanted to know how much went into a show of this scope (if you've never seen "Lights Motors Action", the stage itself was set in a southern French village, so it was pretty darn big). The tour and information I assembled and then delivered was me unintentionally leading by example. After our morning warm-up, which was conducted every day, I arranged to have some of the stunt drivers and moto riders come out and talk to the tour guests. Here, they became celebrities, sharing matter-of-factly what they did on stage. They also got the opportunity to share any TV or film projects they were working on, a question that popped up with every tour. People love this behind-the-scenes knowledge, and every one of these tours created brand ambassadors - people who shared their enthusiasm for the show because they'd been given a peek behind the stage, figuratively and literally. The stunt drivers and motos also become subject matter experts beyond the scope of the stunt skill set proudly on display several times a day.

Because of my drive to do more, and my passion for the brand, I found a space no one knew existed and filled it. I was still a stunt driver, but I found a new opportunity to share my knowledge of the LMA stage show with anyone who was interested. When you know your audience, you can tailor any message to make it relatable. One of the legacies I left for the "Lights Motors Action" stage was a story that could be told after I was gone. When I embarked on my journey into salaried leadership, the LMA tour was a fully capable cast of individuals introducing the show, personalizing each tour with their own knowledge, thoughts, and experiences.

When I became a Disney manager, the first location I landed did not have up-to-date training documents. As mentioned previously, several years had passed since they'd onboarded a new manager. I created a one-sheet that came to be known as the "Day at a Glance" doc, tailored to each operation. I wanted to build a document so simple that even *I* would understand it, even if I knew nothing at all about the new operation and its protocols. At the page's bottom, extensions and contact names were listed, as well as links for various documents and applications used throughout the day. These "Day at a Glance" one-sheets provided an overview for the workday of a manager, whether they were the opening, middle, or closing leader. In short, these sheets were meant to be a guide so that even someone without any experience in a particular operation would still have an idea of what to do. I created a version of this document for every subsequent location where I worked. In compensating for my own needs, I brought value to others.

The best way to contribute to your organization is to study and identify where needs and adjustments can take place. I said *can*, and not *need* or *must*. During my leadership career, one of the resort's executive leaders shared with me a valuable insight. He told me that even though you'll want you make changes immediately, don't. Take notes, write down your questions, and observe instead. In ninety days, you'll have an answer to just about every question, and you'll have been with the operation long enough to understand the culture of accomplishment. Act once you have the blessing of your leadership. Be a team player and watch the opportunities grow. Think in terms of planting a garden. Your ideas are the seeds, and the growth is your actions as a result of the partnerships. A partner to this is how it applies to you. Wherever you land, your first directive should be to bloom where you are planted.

Identifying potentials for self-created opportunities can be either need-based or passion-driven. It can be as simple as asking a manager to requisition a cabinet to stock with snacks and food for employees who forget their lunch, or who wind up extending their shift and need a pick-me-up to get through the rest of the day. With asset management, such things don't cost the operation anything since other areas are constantly looking to re-home everything imaginable. I argued for this idea with a manager, and she was hesitant to implement something she believed would encourage people not to bring their own food. I told her it wouldn't be abused, and when she protested some more, I asked her if she had ever forgotten her lunch, or her keys, or her wallet. I watched her face as she came around. Even if there are the outliers who take advantage of a particular perk or situation, they are vastly outweighed and outnumbered by those who have demonstrated need and appreciation.

There are so many ways you can volunteer to contribute, even with something as simple as offering to come in early and decorate the break room for a particular holiday. There's a good chance extra hours are built into the weekly budget and your manager will give you the thumbs up. Whenever you discover an opportunity to improve an operation's space or logistics, you free up a manager's time to do other things. Plus, it makes them look good and gets you on the radar.

When I was an Entertainment Manager at Epcot, I discovered one of the performers had come up with this wonderful idea called the "Good Note Box". She had repurposed a clear container and cut a slot into the screw top. The instructions were simple. When you wanted to share a positive insight or thought about someone, you would anonymously write it on one of the post-it notes, fold it up and drop it in. When the container was full, one of the entertainment peeps based at the venue would take the lid off and empty the contents onto a table. Then cast members could go through the notes and read them all. This little activity generated many wonderful discoveries about our coworkers, along with many smiles. When I moved on to my next leadership role, one of the performers from the previous stage reached out and asked me to stop by the green room. I ducked in to say hi, and they handed me a folded-up piece of purple paper, addressed to me. When I opened it, I found a neatly written note thanking me for always being there and always being so positive. I was moved, to say the least. This green room had always been a markedly positive space, and it's obvious the people who filled it were a huge part of the reason why.

The second time I went to work at a Six Flags park, it was in another country. Thanks to the relationships I'd built, a friend suggested me for the role and brought me over. Once there, I looked for opportunities to enhance the experience at our show. I worked with the set dressers to fix up and decorate the set behind and beyond the stage. I sat with the audio tech and together we created a load-in and load-out music playlist. When the park manager's son had a birthday coming up, my friend and I designed a fantasy-influenced adventure for the young boy. We weren't asked to do any of these things, but we were both birds of a feather when it came to identifying ways in which to add value to the area. It's less about assessing for opportunities and more about value creation, about thinking and performing beyond the role. Besides, as creatives (he and I are both also writers), it was a natural outlet.

CONTINUE YOUR EDUCATION.

I've always understood and appreciated the importance of an education in all forms. I went back to get my master's degree later in life, and it's always been a priority to stress to my children why education is a necessary pursuit no matter where in life you are. Disney and Universal both emphasize the importance of education with their tuition reimbursement programs. When I started my journey with Disney, they had a college reimbursement program in place that had a few stipulations for access. Still, the fact that the company offered such a program shows they understood the value of investing in their employees. When Disney announced the Aspire program, I encouraged every cast member I knew who was thinking about college to take advantage of it. The Walt Disney Company had smartly replaced their education reimbursement program with this new opportunity where tuition was paid up front, books and other fees were reimbursed, and the catalog of programs continuously expanded and updated.

If you've wanted to pursue a college degree, advanced degree, or certification and find yourself working at a theme park, know that you can (and should) take advantage of any education program offered. Too few companies have anything like this in place. I like to think of Disney's education program as a similar opportunity to investing in a 401(k). In my opinion, people who don't invest in a 401(k) when a company provides a matching option are walking away from money on the table every single week. Your education is a thing that serves you both at Disney and beyond. Plus, with Disney, once you graduate, you get offered membership to the Disney Aspire Alumni Association. Joining is a no-brainer with all the contacts and connections the association guarantees for your future. Today's fellow college graduates are tomorrow's pillars of society and industry. Just like any fraternity or sorority, the Alumni Association creates a vast field of connection opportunities. The Walt Disney Company put a great deal of thought into how to elevate today's employees and create multiple channels for future success.

When it comes to education options in the entertainment arena, Universal and Disney lead the way. I think about the saying, "If you think an education is expensive, try ignorance," because not taking advantage of a tuition reimbursement program is leaving money on the table. Check with your leader or HR, because if you don't want to go after a degree, or another degree, there may be certificates and designations you can pursue that better fit with your personal and career aspirations. The financial assistance for your education is another excellent perk that comes with being a part of these companies, and I'd encourage anyone who is able, to take advantage of it.

<u>BUILD RELATIONSHIPS.</u>

Never underestimate the value of building a relationship.

I'm not talking about networking, which, as a term, has gotten far too much press as the go-to word. I encourage people to replace the word 'networking' with 'bridge'. Personally, I prefer bridge-building. Networks can be tenuous and temporary, but a bridge is designed to support and carry on its mission long after it's created.

Networks are frequently abandoned, but bridges are there for all to maintain and utilize. Networks rely on people to connect; bridges are by virtue connectors. In my two-plus decades at Disney, I had many opportunities to build bridges, to learn, and to grow. My biggest motivation for this was the people I got to work with. In many companies, it's commonplace to build a friendship here and there. In most places, when you are around the same people every day, you tend to build friendly relationships with them, but rarely do you spend extensive amounts of time outside of work with them. At Disney, I wound up making so many friends, that every get-together I host or attended is inevitably filled with fellow cast members. Weddings, birthday parties, cruises, and trips, you name it. The same thing applies to a lesser degree for both Universal and Six Flags (in my personal experience). Relationships at these places endure well beyond the time clock when you spend so much time, day after day, with the same people.

Another perk of these workplace friendships? Many a day off can be spent visiting a theme park or water park where fellow cast members are posted. From day one, Traditions encourages us to create relationships, and maintaining these bonds is as simple as striking up a conversation with the person next to you. Over time, I realized working for Disney subtly changed the way I processed my surroundings. I didn't notice these new perception filters until I spoke with someone who had a similar experience. We both worked for Disney, and we would both weigh, measure, and assess everything from Good Show to customer interactions. We couldn't help it any less than we could help giving directions with the standard two-finger point. Out in the real world, that little habit is the Disney version of a thieves' guild handshake. One can always identify a fellow cast member, present and former, by the way they point when giving someone else directions.

Whenever I reflect on how influential my time at the theme parks was on my personal life, I don't have to look much past my friend group, which is made up primarily of former and current cast members and team members. They live in other towns, other states, and other countries, but no matter how much time goes by, the first thing that happens when I go to visit one of them is a great big hug. That's an incredible greeting from an old work colleague.

Case in point about people and relationships. My time at one of the international Six Flags parks gave me friendships that are closer to being kin. I make it point to visit once a year, that is how close and important these people are.

One of my oldest friends via Disney became a friend even before I went to work for Park Attraction Operations. Kev was a cast member and we connected during one of my park visits, a connection still blazing strong decades later. Along with Kev came Will, another who I keep up with.

Brandon is someone who is very much a brother to me and has been present in my life during the meteoric highs and belly scraping lows. He and I met while he was on college program and we both worked the same attraction. We connected at a deep level, both on and off the clock. He and I spent plenty of time at the Big Bamboo and a few other local hangouts. I sang at their wedding, their daughter was the flower girl at ours. We were groomsman for each other, and every single conversation we have leaves me appreciating the beauty of having this family in my life. They are family to my family as mine is to theirs. Are not these also the kind of relationships you want to build?

Build those relationships. They all matter more than you think.

Friendship as a keystone became one of the main ways I assessed business relations and partnerships. Whenever I meet someone for the first time, I work to get a feel for their personality and character. I asked myself the same question: *is this someone I'd want to hang around if this wasn't a business interaction?* If the answer was no, the individual was likely not someone I wanted to conduct business with. This applies to any workplace environment where partnership is involved and has as much to do with integrity as it does with association. Here's another layer to consider. If you go into a business partnership with someone who has questionable morals, or a take advantage of others business mindset, at some point through association, the perception of others will apply to you. Nothing can tarnish a reputation faster than association.

Some people may disagree with this and believe that business relationships are a completely different beast. I once heard someone say, "Business is business, so don't take it personally, and don't let it get personal." I do not agree, because a business relationship on its own is a standalone transactional relationship and you need the personal cues to take it further. If that was not the case, theme parks would have worn out their welcome long ago and not enjoyed the multigenerational activity of entire families who plan annual visits to share the magic and create new memories. People leave jobs because of people, not because of the company. As a consumer, most of the time this is also the case. That is worth pondering. Families will take on debt just to revisit and recreate an experience, whether it is going to the same park or staying at the same resort. They want reassurance and a certain comfort for the soul that will not happen if it is strictly a business exchange. I met a couple who got engaged at the "Hoop Dee Doo Revue". They come back every year, staying at the same resort, and have stayed in touch with many of the same cast members who have been supporting players in their journey over the past twenty-six years since they got engaged. That's relationship building at its finest. On the other side of that coin, I have friends who are entertainers who share with me how humbling it is that a family will plan their visit around them, and when they'll be working. As crazy as it sounds, that is the power of relationships.

Building relationships throughout your personal and professional universe can help you avoid some of the potholes and speed bumps your role deficiencies might bring along. Just as any Michael Jordan was not a Michael Jordan at the start of their careers, every great leader must learn through experiences, challenges, and mistakes. Every VP, EVP, and CEO started out as an entry-level manager. Before that, many of them started as hourly employees. We might all think we know best whenever we undertake a new endeavor, but only an infinitesimal number of us actually do. The hours of action we burn is the experience we earn, and part of that experience comes from paying attention to the right people and the right messages.

Here's one example: not a month into my first leadership assignment, I found myself getting frustrated by what I saw as shortsighted and inefficient decision-making. During one of my park walks, I had identified a vacant space for which I thought there could be better uses that would serve our team, but no one seemed to be responding when I reached out with the idea. After not hearing back from any stakeholders for two weeks, I sent an 11:00 p.m. email to my leader that started with what I believed was a subtle opener. "Help me to understand," as it turns out, was anything but subtle. The email went on much longer than necessary. I got a response at 2:15 *in the morning*. His reply? "I have you on my calendar for an 8:15 AM meeting. See you then."

I showed up at his office, and he asked me to close the door. Roy, my leader, is as warm and affable as they come, yet as I looked at him I was not sure what was coming next. My name plaque hadn't yet arrived. As you know, this was my very first official leadership role, and it would be embarrassing if I was summarily kicked off the team after less than a month. He told me he had wanted me on the team because I brought a different perspective. He sensed I was willing to challenge convention, and I was new blood in an old operational body. He confided after getting my email that he was glad to see he wasn't wrong about me. Having said all of that, he told me there's a right way and a wrong way to say things, especially at Disney. He quickly and correctly assessed that I hadn't developed my leadership filters yet. He explained that the way I began my email might have caused someone else to bristle. The lesson? It's one we've all been taught. Consider your words carefully.

He followed that with several pieces of advice, advice I still leverage to this day:

1) If you're going to send an email, let it sit for a little bit before hitting send. If you decide you want to send it, you should read it over again and make sure there's no room for misinterpretation. If you can physically talk to that person, face to face, do that instead.

2) It's important to learn as much about an operation as possible before you start challenging or questioning why things happen the way they do.

3) Ask yourself if there is a better way to say something. If there is, use it. You are always working to build an army of advocates, and when you put people on the defensive in a corporate environment, it takes a long time for them to change their way of thinking.

4) Think about how you would want the message you are delivering to be delivered to you.

5) Trust but Verify.

Those five short pieces of wisdom are an excellent foundation to building your professional relationships. They were for me. At the time, I still didn't understand, but as I advanced in my leadership journey, the importance of what my manager said to me that day gradually sunk in. I also began to appreciate how my manager was exactly right for that role, and I was beyond thankful he'd taken an interest in me and my professional development.

Another good example of relationship building involves the conversations I had with GMs and VPs. The first time I had a sit-down meeting with a much higher up, I immediately asked, "How do I get to where you are?"

Dan Cockerell, the VP seated across from me, nodded. "You should start by asking the right questions; that is not the right question." His answer sounded like a needle scratch across an LP to me. I came in confident and cocky, and this man, a Disney Legacy Leader, elected to steer me with a gentleness I hadn't yet developed. We went on to have a great conversation about personal development. Those conversations continued anytime he saw me out in the park. He encouraged me to lean into other people and situations. When you take care of your people and they take care of the operation, everything works out.

When I was a leader at Epcot, I got onto our Entertainment General Manager's (GM) calendar as soon as I could. His name was Greg (Disney is a first-name company, from hourly all the way up to CEO). I told him I wanted to grow my career in the company and was thinking of getting my master's degree because I didn't see how it could hurt. He agreed that without such degrees, there was a limit in the current climate as to how much one could rise through the company ranks. Greg told me an MBA was great, but a Master's degree in any discipline demonstrated dedicated focus and commitment to personal development. In other words, such a degree allows any candidate under consideration to pass the litmus test.

Then he told me to listen more and talk less.

New managers always have ideas and want to share them, eagerly grabbing for the rudder to steer the ship. The problem with that, Greg said, is that a new manager doesn't know the hazards under water and is only going to run aground. Failure is a part of learning, but realistically, you want to do as little of it as possible. The failures you encounter become teachable moments. When you become a new manager in a theme park operation, you are forced to get uncomfortable, and that discomfort can sometimes feel like facing off against the firehose of knowledge. Paying attention is the only way to keep from drowning. As with any skill set, it gets easier once you find the things that transfer. As an hourly, the learning opportunities and hazards are no different.

In the years that followed, I found myself paying attention to the leaders I admired most. I was always paying attention; I simply adjusted my focus. These leaders did, in fact, seem intent on listening more, and they took every single thing they heard into consideration. As new managers, our own ideas seem novel; for the leader listening to us, it's the fourth time that month someone has pitched the same thing without understanding the logistics behind why it isn't viable. I'm not suggesting you keep your ideas to yourself. Do what another GM recommended to me. Get a small notebook or use the notepad feature on your phone. For the first two to three months of your managerial assignment, every time something sparks an idea or criticism of an existing system, write it down. Greg was another executive who reminded me of this process. He suggested that at the end of the first ninety days, most of the questions would answer themselves. Greg had been with the company for over thirty years and worked at both Disneyland and the Walt Disney World Resort, always employing this process when he landed in a new line of business. The "talk less, listen and smile more" advice had always been hard for me (as it is for many top 10% people on the 10/80/10 scale), but taking notes when I was the new manager on the block always served me well… once I conditioned myself to actually do this.

Another great piece of advice I got? Make it fun. One day, I was walking through our admin building. I ducked my head into our GM's office as I walked past. She invited me in, and we talked for a few minutes. During our chat, I asked her what the most important thing to her was as a Disney hourly cast member, and how had that changed now that she was a senior leader? She told me the most important thing remained the same. Whenever possible, keep it interesting and keep it fun.

She reminded me that even the most enjoyable job, task, or hobby in the world came with associated activities that are frequently, let's be honest, a drag. She also said something I hadn't considered before: it's always possible to suck the fun out of something, and just because something was enjoyable in the past didn't automatically mean it would be so again. Letting individuals find the why behind what they're doing, sometimes with coaching and encouragement from you as a leader, allows them to maintain the fun. We are wired to perform better when we understand the drivers and motivations behind our goals. When you understand the why, you're able to keep the getting there fun for yourself and everyone else.

My GM used entertainment and theater as an example. For every person who doesn't enjoy the audition part of the process, there's someone else who thrives on it. The same applies to learning your lines, learning your choreography, your blocking, building sets, running audio or lighting, directing, and stage managing. One person cannot imagine anything other than being on stage, while the next person wants nothing to do with being on stage, yet they both love the theater space equally. Two individuals can find elevated joy in different parts of a process, and that is always because of mindset.

The addendum? When you find a way to identify and elevate the joy in each element of your day, the people working alongside you will want a part of it. This is never a bad thing. Quite the opposite, it's the best place for you to find yourself. Every action we take can create value. It all depends on us and our perspective. When we keep it fun and interesting for ourselves and others, everybody benefits. If you enjoy what you do, you never work a day in your life. That is an elemental truth. Add to this the ability to observe, listen, and process, and no matter where you go, you have created a permanent recipe for learning and continued success.

Relationship building is an essential part of life, whether we're talking about work or personal life. In your career, you come to understand that your professional development is as much influenced by others as it is by yourself. Nothing is a straightforward, linear track, it's more like a slow game of chess where new pieces and levels are constantly being added. At home, it is rare to find someone who hasn't had a conversation with their significant other where the exclamatory, "Well, why didn't you tell me this before!" or "Oh, now I understand!" didn't make an appearance. Everything is about growing stronger by understanding the expectations we impose on ourselves, and how we grow by overcoming or adapting to our limitations. For 99% of us, this comes from strengthening our bonds to others.

Just as we have work mentors, we rely on the informed insight of those emotionally closest to us to provide direction. Not a single one of us is on this journey alone. The tip of the iceberg only looks like the most important part because it's the most immediately visible, but it's everything underneath that provides support and elevation.

Relationship building is important to every operation. Many of today's GMs, VPs, and other executives in any theme park enterprise started out as busboys, servers, attraction hosts, and entertainment performers. This is a remarkable constant not only with the Disney organization, but in many theme parks. In every case, these individuals did not get to their executive roles by themselves. If it takes a village to raise a child, it takes a team to build a leader.

There is no such thing as a 'self made anything. We get where we seek to go sometimes on the shoulders of giants, and oftentimes because of those around us who leverage their own experiences to help us gain ours. Given that relationships are such an important piece of the puzzle (and why it is listed as the closing topic here), I want to end this chapter by talking about some specific people who offered invaluable insight, and beyond this, built formative relationships with me. These relationships continue to profoundly impact me in positive ways for which I am still gaining benefit.

Sheri: I met Sheri when I started the second chapter of my Disney journey, at the stunt show. She was a show producer who had already been with the company for quite a long time. We become close enough to the point where I'd schedule appointments, mostly to just stop by her office and catch up. There were plenty of times where I would just swing by her office and if she was available, she would drop what she was doing to chat. She always provided tremendous insight and direction for me, both professionally and personally. Sherry tried to get me to go into entertainment leadership years before I made the move; As Thoreau wrote, I was the typical example of every man who marched to the beat of his own drummer. When I finally made the move, she cautioned me on the challenges new leaders often encountered and advised me on how to best mitigate them. Our personal connection remains strong, and we stay in touch to this day.

Chris: Chris and I met when I was doing "The Wild Wild Wild West Stunt Show" at Universal. I had been trained up as Brett Taylor, and he was one of the Cole Hoppers, the bad guy role. We connected one day between shows, while setting props and prepping the stage for the next performance (in most live shows, and almost always in film and TV, the stunt men and women are the people giving a final eye over the sets they're going to perform on since their lives depend on everything being set up properly). Chris did other shows at Universal and talked about living overseas. I listened to these stories with great interest. One day he said to me, "If I go back to Holland as stunt captain, and I bring my own team, you're first on my list." Listen - if I got a job every time someone said something along those lines to me, I would never have had a day off. But Chris was a man of his word and called me up one day asking if I wanted to go to the Netherlands. So began my love affair with the Netherlands and my appreciation that someone like Chris existed in the entertainment industry, someone who lived by their word.

Wendy: I got to know Wendy at DPI, my very first management assignment. As a stunt performer, I recognized her from the stage because she swung by on a regular basis and affectionately referred to the stunt performers as "hot pockets" because of our tailored driving suits. I loved going by her office to see how things were going in her world. In getting to know her, I discovered a warm and tremendously gregarious individual, highly knowledgeable about the underpinnings of both the entertainment operation and the mechanics of decision-making across the whole park. It harkened back to my time in film and TV, where knowing people in craft services got you both wild stories and glimpses of production company insight, as well as hints into what was coming your way next. Wendy had stories aplenty, but she also provided perspective on the operation itself, the perspective from someone who saw and understood everything happening around her. She provided constant peek-behind-the-curtain insights. Although she and her husband moved out of state, we still happily keep in touch to this day.

Paul: Paul and I immediately hit it off at the "Lights Motors Action" stunt show. He was part of the tech team, and I was a driver, and none of that mattered. On some stages there is an unwritten caste system in place. Performers at the top, with tech and operations close to the bottom. This was not the case for our stage, perhaps because we were physically and culturally insulated from the rest of the park. Whatever the case, I am grateful. The techs were with us from day one. Paul and I discovered a mutual passion for Walt Disney the man. We also have a mutual fondness for 20,000 Leagues, Fort Wilderness, and Royal Caribbean. We cemented our bond after my trip to Disneyland Paris, where I went on a photo safari to visit the 20,000 Leagues submarine, the Nautilus, life-size and sitting in the middle of a moat. I came back with framed pictures, eliciting the desired enthusiastic response from Paul. When I started building the Amazing Race style tours for our stage, I relied on his help to do the research and add the right details. Our relationship with our managers allowed us to conduct these projects independent of oversight. As I've said before, when you build any relationship on a foundation of trust and integrity, your leadership team knows they don't have to watch over your shoulder. As a connector, Paul stands in a league all his own. We spend all the time we can together, especially if that time involves rocking chairs in front of Crockett's Tavern.

Caroline: Caroline was in VIP Tours when I met her during Take Two of my Traditions audition. Traditions, as you may recall, is Disney's version of orientation. To this day, it was one of the most demanding auditions I have ever had, a multi-layered and multileveled trial by fire, an experience I would happily repeat in a heartbeat. Caroline and I connected right away at the second audition and first callback. Our passion for Disney, the man and his vision, was on full display. There were two other people in that callback, but neither Caroline nor I could tell you who they were, in part because we had such an instant rapport that we were busy leaping in to finish each other's sentences whenever the panel posed a question. That callback ran like a joint interview for the two of us.

She and I connected on such a level that, when we saw each other at the fourth callback, we immediately hugged. We remained close through our year and a half with Traditions and beyond. So connected were we, in fact, that when there were Traditions shifts that needed coverage, we would reach out to see if the other was free to facilitate, so we could teach together. She's one of the most amazing and positive people I've ever met, pixie dust in human form. Every time we get together, it's like sitting at the portal of enlightenment with someone so much wiser.

There's a group of us from Traditions who still stay in touch. During our eighteen months as facilitators, we met up about once a month to socialize, or do a brand awareness tour, or simply catch up. Then we formed a softball team because that core group of us simply couldn't get enough of each other. We all walked away so much better for the experience.

Nannette: I met Nanette when I got hired back to Disney as part of the opening team for "Lights Motors Action". She was with us from the very beginning, when we were training at the Wonders Lot under cloak and dagger circumstances. We were sharing driving suits and Nomex (fire retardant material that looks like thermal underwear, worn underneath the driving suit) because we didn't have enough of either. Every day, we would show up at 7:30 a.m. and all our costumes would be cleaned and ready to go. When we repositioned to the stage, we had a much later call time. Not me. I started coming in early, and I'm thankful the management team allowed me to do so (by Disney policy, employees are not *supposed* to show up until fifteen minutes before the start of their shift. Most companies, theme park operators included, have similar policies in place). Our call time was sixty minutes before warm-up to guarantee that the stage had the staffing to do a show, but I would show up ninety minutes to two hours beforehand. Early is on time, and on time is late, right?

I'd catch up with the managers, and then I'd grab coffee and sit down with Nannette. We chatted over our respective warm mugs until it was time for me to start show warm-up. We had to go through costuming to get our gear for the show, and I would always notice the racks of nice dress clothes and polo shirts the actors wore. Nannette approached me one day after the show had been open for a few months and told me about the discard process. She explained that old clothes would be cycled out and tossed. She asked if I was interested in any of them. The actors on the stage all wore street clothes, but every one of those items were costuming department bought and approved. New clothes were purchased on a regular basis. She knew by looking that my body type and physique matched a couple of the performers. As you might've guessed, Disney doesn't shop at a discount clothier. Thanks to Nannette, I wound up with a nice collection of shirts and pants. She not only kept me safe with my personal protective equipment, but she prevented me from looking like a complete slouch by keeping me reasonably well dressed, too.

Eric: Eric and I had known each other from film projects before Disney. Working together at the stunt show allowed us to bond at a deeper level. I have worked with him on a variety of projects, including a national commercial where he got me my SAG card (Screen Actors Guild). We talk on a regular basis, meeting up as frequently as our schedules allow. In the film and TV industry, he is one of the few individuals who clearly epitomizes integrity. He's highly regarded for his subject matter expertise and respected as a penultimate safety professional. Early on, when I started action coordinating film and TV projects, he was always there to help me see the things I might've missed. Whether we're talking about Disney, the financial markets (he is an investment wiz also) or a big budget film project, I've always been able to count on his insight. When I was looking to interview for various mid and senior level positions at Disney, he always seemed to have a contact to help provide me additional perspective. We have spent enough time together that our daughters have played together. I wouldn't trade my relationship with him for anything in the world.

Lloyd: If you're lucky, you get to work for a company where you find someone to study and learn from. You marvel and become amazed at how unflappable this person is. You decide that if you ever go into management, you want to be just like them. They inspire you. Lloyd is that person for me.

I connected with Lloyd when I was doing LMA. He was our park area leader and an ever-present figure around the green room. When I started looking for ways to increase my value, I approached him. When I wanted to facilitate Traditions, he was right there to encourage me, right up to the point where the reveal happened, and I found out I made the team. It was August, and I was in a two-piece suit standing in the Magic Kingdom, a hot, crying, sweaty mess. Lloyd was right there with a balloon, a congratulations, and that much-needed hug. He was good at keeping a secret because he knew more than two weeks before I did.

I wanted to do "On With the Show", Disney's Hollywood Studios orientation experience. I had ideas on how to improve and dress up the Greenroom at LMA. I wanted to place holiday decor all over the building façade of our stage. I wanted to build a tour for Disney University. In all cases, Lloyd would give me a green light and simply say, "Keep me in the loop." When the stage had to go dark for resurfacing, he gave me the go ahead after I suggested building a heritage and legacy day for the cast. When I wanted to come over to resorts, he was the proprietor who brought me over, setting me up for success as a stage manager for the "Hoop Dee Doo Revue" in Pioneer Hall at Fort Wilderness and the "Spirit of Aloha Dinner Show", an authentic Luau that took place in Luau Cove at the Polynesian resort. I learned and managed other shows as well, all because of him. Lloyd has been a constant presence, always my advocate, yet careful to let me stumble and learn. We stay in touch and get together for breakfast or lunch when the opportunity presents itself.

They may be many, but this list is not complete. There was also people like Diane, my show director at Universal, who took the time to help me develop by having career conversations with me. Leaders like Matt and Carmen, who taught me the value and importance of an open-door policy. Andy and Jeremy, who not only taught me the value of an open-door policy, but endured hours upon hours of me coming to the stage early, grabbing coffee, and planting myself in their office. Not hyperbole at all. I'd usually come in two to three hours early, find the manager's door open, see Jeremy trying to get caught up on an impossibly growing slew of emails, while doing Workbrain (how the several dozen performers on the stage got paid), and would greet me as I walked into the office. And we'd talk. About everything.

Every one of these examples highlight how relationships can take many forms, just as they can carry you in many different directions. All you have to do is get to know people and let them get to know you. There are few ways to build traction on the road to professional growth as enjoyable as this.

Several years into my leadership journey, I had the opportunity to go back and sit down with my first leader, Roy. I apologized to him for being a pain in the ass while on his team. He laughed and shook his head, then told me he wouldn't have had it any other way. He said the company needed people like me, passionate and eager, not jaded or beaten down. He told me the challenging parts of my personality were what made me an attribute to pretty much any organization. I just had to learn how to develop my filter to deploy these traits effectively. He thanked me for always being willing to listen and sticking it out. New managers sometimes burn out quickly because they get frustrated when the experience isn't as advertised. I had to learn how to manage my own reins, not nearly as easy as it sounds. Plus, I had to learn this while learning how to manage a team, difficult when people lean into you because of these inherent leadership skills they believe you possess even if you yourself don't yet feel as confident. Fellow peers like Monalee and Mike fanned the flames of servant leadership in me. Treated as an equal, they taught me much, such as paying attention to everything when doing a park walk. I carried that initiative into every subsequent leadership assignment. They are also of the old school building-connections-that-matter mindset. More than peers, like so many of my theme park connections, they remain friends to this day.

I knew exactly why I was in leadership. It wasn't to change processes (even if, during this journey, I would question processes all the time). I was committed to making a difference through relationships.

No matter what you do, no matter what company or organization you wind up with, if leadership is in your forward-looking horizon, relationships are how anything and everything get done. At any theme park, this is a part of the journey you can look forward to. For me, that journey made itself known at the Walt Disney World Resort in Orlando, Florida. It is not unreasonable to think the idea of relationship building is something Walt Disney himself knew was important, something that would exist and outlast him. Just as the park will always grow and change, the people who bring everything to life will build relationships that benefit everyone and everything.

When you work at a theme park, the relationships you build become part of your legacy. People will always remember how you made them feel, so make those relationships count in their quality and caliber.

SO...YOU WORKED AT A THEME PARK

When I started my journey with Disney for the first time (like so many cast and crew members, I left the Disney fold only to return later), I'd interviewed several times. I was delicately told, "Thanks, but no thanks." And then, one time, my time came. Before my first "yes", I had auditioned repeatedly. I could not and did not give up. That's a general life lesson: if you want something, you have to decide how much you want the thing and then put in all the effort you can into making it happen.

My Universal story was dramatically different. I had been to the park once, when there was only one park, for a grand opening. I went to the Universal audition while still working at Disney (which is not taboo - quite the opposite, there is a tremendous amount of cross-population for performers and other hourly roles between the two). I walked into the audition room for "The Wild Wild Wild West Stunt Show" and greeted the people behind the table. With the pleasantries out of the way, I expected to launch right into my monologue.

But that did not happen. When Adrian asked me, in a BBC1 British accent, if I'd ever fallen off a horse, I wish I could say I was trying to be funny with my response. That wasn't the case. My, "Not intentionally," was a very matter-of-fact statement. I didn't pass myself off as an expert - I knew which part of the horse was the front end and which was the back end, and I knew how to make the animal go forward and park, most of the time. I had enough experience growing up around horses to know, as with motorcycles, that it isn't a matter of if you fall off, but when. It happens to everyone. When you tack up a horse and don't remember to check the girth strap for snugness, or neglect to cast an investigating eye over the animal to see if they're holding their breath (because horses have a funny sense of humor like that), you can count on falling off sooner rather than later.

When I left Disney, my film and television career was starting to take off. I landed roles at Universal with "The Wild Wild Wild West Stunt Show" and "T-2: Terminator 3D". I'd booked roles in film and TV on projects like *From the Earth to the Moon, Armageddon,* and *Burn Notice*. I was booking work in other parts of the state, other states, and even other countries. Disney was growing further and further in my rearview mirror. That was never intentional. I always maintained a very simple metric for staying with Disney: as long as it's fun, I'll stick around. With Disney, it was fun for a tremendously long time, but as other things started to compete for my attention, it became difficult to maintain my status with the company. I knew I had to give something up, and as much as I never thought I could, I decided it was time to get out of the way and let other people make Disney magic. I was thankful for my time and grateful for the friendships I made, some of which would endure for decades. I was grateful for having built relationships with some of the managers, who always agreed to let me pick up shifts regardless of my status. It would be difficult to leave, but with a budding film and

TV career, I also couldn't be in two places at once. I was starting to feel the sleep deprivation of trying to creeping in. It reminded me of my start in college. In my first semester, I worked a full-time day job, kept a full-time school schedule with twelve credit hours, and I had an early morning job several mornings a week. Sleep was something that happened to other people. The exact same thing was happening to me now. There were days I started at Universal, went to Disney (or vice versa), and then had a late production call. It's great to be busy, but at some point, sacrifices had to be made for long term success and sanity.

Before leaving Disney/MGM Studios, I spent a long while reflecting on my journey at the House of the Mouse. Beginning to end, it was nowhere near as straightforward as my Universal path. When I got hired for Disney attractions operations, I lived in South Florida. I went up to interview and audition at the encouragement of Lee, the mother of a close friend. She knew my history with Disney, namely trying to get hired and failing. She told me told me to try again anyway, confident I would get the gig. When they finally offered me a role, I continued to live in South Florida for another two years, commuting. With a three-hour trip each way, if I had a shift that started at eight in the morning, I'd leave at four AM to get to the park. For a long time, I would stay overnight at an inexpensive hotel on 192. It was a family-owned enterprise that would've probably done a brisk business if they rented by the hour, but they gave me a break because I stayed there one or two nights a week.

At "Inside the Magic", it started with me offering to pick up the end of people's shifts if they wanted an early release (ER). Soon enough, my fellow cast members would come and ask me if I wanted the rest of their shift, or even a shift for the next day. I quickly developed a reputation as someone who would pick up or extend on a shift, no matter what it was. I've talked about relationship building previously, and it certainly applied here. I always made sure that I came in early and did more than expected. I never once had a manager object to extending me. In fact, one holiday season, I picked up so many shifts I wound up working an eighty-hour week. It was mutually beneficial: good for the operation and good for me (if entirely fatiguing). Ron the attractions cast member learned a great deal about himself during that week.

When I learned the script for the sound stages, I did some of my own research. I'll never forget one of my sound stage tours being evaluated or the response afterward. Disney's quality control back then was fairly exhaustive. Each area and line of business creates its own protocols to ensure everything they produce is up to standard. This goes for everything from a tour to a Dole Whip. Their standards will stay as demanding as they were the first day of operations. For any attraction with spieling, quality control is managed by the show evaluation team, who are typically Imagineers, and part of Disney Creative. More often than not, these are the individuals who did more than just deliver the script to a venue. They wrote the script, or even more, they created the venue in the first place. After one evaluation, the cast member conducting the overview came to me afterward and asked me how I knew so much about the production side of things. *From the Earth to the Moon* had been filming on two of the four sound stages, and I had spent a great deal of time on them. I told her I was delivering on personal experiences. She got very excited and nodded. "We should all be talking about this. The fact that our studio is a working production facility is a pretty neat talking point." I agreed.

To this day, it holds true that people have a deep fascination with production work, especially what takes place behind the scenes. Kris, the young woman who did my show evaluation, handed me the eval form. It showed my strengths, weakness, and where I could improve. I had one small opportunity for improvement. She suggested that when I had really small audiences, I draw them in close and not use a microphone. Besides that, she enjoyed everything, adding "pleasant deviation to script" under her 'additional notes' section. That was a big deal for me. Even then I wanted to prove that I was worthy of wearing the Disney name tag every single day. Another time my evaluation was conducted by Paul. I always believed his was a talent wasted in our theme park world - with his voice, looks and presence, the man belonged on Broadway. He told me the most interesting parts of my tour were the elements that I introduced from personal experience, something I had heard before. He also appreciated how I successfully managed to weave in the necessary talking points, making the presentation vastly personal and relatable. The lesson here is simple. You never know how risks you take to improve an operation will play out until they're

executed, but you will never see the results if you don't
take the risks to begin with.

How badly do you want something? It never hurts to
pull that card and let the people behind the desk know.
The stories of your experiences, your interviews, and
how you overcame adversity? These are the kind of
stories that are worth sharing - not just in an interview,
but with anyone who can't figure out how to create a
highlight reel of their career or get through that difficult
slump. Where other people were willing to do the bare
minimum, I always rolled up my sleeves and made sure
I was there for as long as I needed to be. At Disney, there
were times when I would get to stay for fireworks watch
at the end of my regular shift. This meant being on the
clock in a backstage area and seeing the fireworks from
a completely different perspective. It meant learning
about the safety protocols. It meant being part of the
magic while seeing the magic in action. It meant
building relationships. At Universal, when I was closing
cast for T2, I would stick around and talk to some of the
maintenance crew, watching them cycle the show
elements. Sometimes, they would share which of these
caused the greatest amount of aggravation. At the top
and bottom of the day, like any dark ride or attraction,
the public-facing spaces of this performance venue felt
very different with the work lights on. At Disney, I built
relationships that mattered. I loved what I did. It didn't
matter whether I was standing in the center of the
"Inside the Magic" prop room, talking about special
effects, or sitting in the seat of a "Lights Motors Action"

Opel Corsa, 2-wheeling across the stage. The exuberance experienced was similar.

When I chose to close the chapter of my time as an attractions host and move on to a new page, it felt like the right time. Never in a million years could I have guessed I would wear a Disney name tag again. I couldn't fathom returning to the company as a whole, let alone to the very same park. You see, even though my attractions role was more than a job, it was still *also* a job. What could Disney possibly offer that would cause me to return? In addition to the live stunt shows I was doing at Universal, I was booking increasing amounts of work with motion pictures and TV shows. With the expanse of opportunity that a film and television stunt career held for me, I didn't see any way Disney might appear back in the picture. I figured the only way I'd be back was if I was in one of their films, like *Pirates of the Caribbean* (as it turned out, I got a call to work in the franchise, but I had to turn it down because of other commitments - namely a certain Disney stunt show involving cars and motorcycles). In the interim, I labored to leverage the professional relationships I had built and manicured. In many businesses, who you know is as important as what you know, sometimes more so.

I originally went to work for Disney because it was my dream. I certainly wasn't getting rich. The wealth and riches were coming in the way of experiences, but experiences didn't put gas in the tank or food on the table. Still, I was so ridiculously enthusiastic both backstage and onstage that it was easy for a manager to justify extending me. One of my managers once told me the operation was budgeted for overtime every single day, and if the money did not get spent, they wouldn't get it in the next fiscal year. I got approved for overtime anytime I asked for it. With all the extra work, I managed to save money. This is something to consider. It may be exhausting, but if you have access to overtime, take it. Even with the joy that walking through the park brought me, the fact I made double as a stunt performer at Universal also got my attention. So too when I would be on a film set and get a pay bump or adjustment. I was getting opportunities outside of Disney that were paying well and kept me within my entertainment wheelhouse.

It made me sad to consider my time with Disney was over, but after five years in attractions operations, these opportunities made apparent that it was time to step aside and let other people create pixie dust. During my time at Disney, I learned to develop my listening skills. I learned to ask the right questions and look for opportunities. I learned to take charge and make decisions where guest service recovery was concerned. I developed the confidence to pitch venue ideas to management. I also learned how to lean forward and become a problem solver. One more bonus? I made a bunch of friends, many of whom I remain friends with to this day.

Even though I was an hourly cast member when I left Disney, I was starting to emulate the traits of a good leader. I lived my dream of being a Disney cast member, and it left me shining from the inside out. I learned more than just scripts to spiel to guests. I learned opening and closing responsibilities for a multi-million-dollar attraction. I learned how to apply the Keys for a positive guest experience, the safety protocols of sweeping

Mickey Avenue, and securing the Backlot area. I went from being someone with a limited skillset to a finely tuned individual empowered with a host of responsibilities, some of them key holder in nature. People who criticize the entry level pay at the theme parks miss the finer point: you get hired and trained. There is no limit to the training you have access to. This is like a university master's program that you get paid to attend. For me, there was nothing wrong with the pay scale when considering the other perks that came along with the job.

When I left Universal, it was under similar circumstances. My first role found me on a horse with "The Wild Wild Wild West Stunt Show". Through that show, I built relationships and friendships like the one that brought me to Europe for a year. When I returned, I was back in the saddle, so to speak. As a T-1000 at "T2: 3D - Battle Across Time", I went through remedial training due to blocking and equipment changes but was quickly performing full speed at both shows.

As my film and TV career started to make greater demands of me, coupled with a return to Disney full-time, I was finding myself with less time than ever. You can show up as an attractions host or a food and beverage server with a lack of sleep, but going into a stunt show sleep-deprived is a recipe for disaster. Leaving Universal was sad and difficult, especially since it had launched the live stunt show part of my career, but when it happened, it was time.

When it comes time (and oftentimes you will just know), I encourage you to be okay with your decision to leave. Give yourself grace when questioning why you are leaving. Sometimes there are elements out of your control. Sometimes it's simply time to move on. It can be like the very first time you rode your favorite theme park ride. You board, experience the visceral assault of sensory overload, then process everything as you disembark. If they let you stay on to ride again, it is the same ride. Some elements might stand out differently, but it is still the same. If you feel it is time to move on, that's okay. Remember: the point of departure is the line beyond our comfort zone, and what we do with it is the first step to new growth. Eckhart Tolle says it elegantly with this quote, "What a caterpillar calls the end of the world we call a butterfly." Growth requires constant evolving.

Having said all that, I did end up returning to Disney, this time as a cast member and stuntman on the opening team for "Lights Motors Action - Extreme Stunt Show!" I was every bit as excited going through the interview and audition process this time as I had been every time before, but I was reminded that Disney was still very, very picky and particular when it comes to hiring. They have a brand to protect, and they have an exceptional standard of customer service rivaled in the theme park world perhaps only by Universal. Whether one gets hired as a part-time, full-time, or seasonal, only about one in every five to seven who interview are offered a role.

With the stunt show? Even with the growing success of my acting and stunt career, I had to audition more than once, demonstrating competency in the vehicle while showing I could also listen to direction and take notes. I needed to do all sorts of things I had never done intentionally before, like drifting around a mark, high-speed reverses between two rows of cones without knocking anything over, and ninety degree slides. Reaction time was tested. After three auditions and call backs, I had the opportunity to work with the audition team for the Florida auditions, which I used to my advantage, watching the best and worst performers, and seeing that it wasn't just ability but also attitude that opened doors. I was a quick learner and made sure to apply everything I observed to give me the best possible chance.

The opening cast of performers was twenty-six people, with an additional twelve sub drivers. The audition process saw over five thousand auditionees. The hiring and evaluation team traveled the country and responded to queries from all over the world, offering invitations to audition to those they found qualified. They provided location and vehicles and were always critical in their assessments. They had to be. Disney had never done a show in the U.S. with the potential for so much to go wrong as this one.

In general terms, both Disney and Universal select the best of the best. Looking at a few of their live productions, such as "Beauty and the Beast", "The Wild Wild Wild West Stunt Show", "Hunchback of Notre Dame", "Dynamite Nights Stunt Spectacular", "The Indiana Jones Epic Stunt Spectacular", "Voyage of the Little Mermaid", "T2: 3D - Battle Across Time", "The Hoop Dee Doo Revue", and "Lights Motors Action: Extreme Stunt Show!", two things consistently stand out. One: the respective theme park brand mounted an impressive show. Two: each named show has launched film, TV, Broadway, and touring production careers for many of their performers. Actors, actresses, and stunt performers who all got their start or bolstered their experience points at a theme park moved on to performing, coordinating, and directing in all of these other mediums. Many of the blockbuster films you have seen, chock full of action, will likely have stuntmen and stuntwomen who performed at Disney or Universal. Martial arts coordinators and stunt coordinators emerged from "The Wild Wild Wild West Stunt Show". Stunt drivers from "Lights Motors Action" moved on to the Fast and Furious movie franchise. Action and stunt coordinators came out of the lagoon show, "Dynamite Nights Stunt Spectacular" at Universal, and Indiana Jones stunt actors appear in the Pirates of the Caribbean franchise, among others. One of the guys from LMA landed a role on a global touring Fast and Furious stunt show. The cast had thirteen people and only one American. The fact that he came from our stage says a great deal not only of the hiring procedure that got him there, but also of the talent that stage developed in addition to his existing skill set. Many theme park and live show performers go on to work with actors as their stunt doubles (myself included). Opportunities are endless.

So, the big question: What does working for a theme park do for you and your résumé? Coming out of Disney and Universal, a great deal. On both the acting and stunt side of things, many performers go on to work in Hollywood or climb the ranks of the film and television industry throughout the country and the world - not only performing, but also on the production side of things with equipment set up, assisting and coordinating, or directing the second units (the action film units). Stunt performers can become part of the utility stunt team for a TV series. Actors land day roles, recurring roles, and lead roles in series. Many of yesterday's theme park stunt players are stunt coordinating big budget blockbusters today.

Maybe you never jumped off a building and want to know more about the acting aspect of theme park work, especially how that leads to the next Big Thing. Actors, singers, show hosts, and dancers from theme park productions go on to do a plethora of incredible things. Show director, talk show host, TV series regular, cruise ship act, and Broadway performer are just a few of the roles theme park actors have stepped into after leaving the comfortable bonds of Universal or Disney. Using your favorite search engine to learn more, you might be surprised at the scope of such talent, and even more surprised at their theme park origins.

You might wonder why someone would leave such a gig as theme park work. There's an interesting term within the theme park industry for entertainers and their position. It's called the velvet handcuffs. Working in theme park entertainment is consistent and familiar. Therein exists the challenge. Many actors become unnerved at the idea of giving up the comfort of their daily gig. Anyone protected by an Actors Equity Association collective bargaining agreement at Disney must sit down for contract talks once a year. At Universal, even without the union, the same thing applies. Usually, if you have demonstrated your value and possess a dynamite attitude backstage and onstage, you do not have to worry too much about the park renewing your contract. Getting trained up in other areas amplifies your value both inside the company and beyond.

Speaking of going beyond, I know plenty of people with every sort of theme park background, who have used that experience to build their careers beyond. Trainers at Disney have gone on to education administration. Content developers become consultants. Imagineers become designers. Adventures by Disney guides become concierge travel advisors. YES (Youth Education) facilitators create programs for companies seeking to elevate their own engagement measurements. Attractions hosts become writers, creating fantasy stories about an alternate universe theme park world where people live. The point here is your theme park journey is a starting point for whatever comes next.

As an hourly cast member or team member, it can be a seat of comfort to remain in the same attraction, year after year. You build seniority, you get your pay bumps, and if you are lucky enough to have set up a retirement profile, you feed that as well. But when it is time to go, it's time. I've quite a few friends who moved on, retiring from Universal or Disney. I know a few who went back. Everyone has their own story to tell.

Taking on managerial duties and responsibilities was, for me, essential to developing my long-term career. As a manager or team leader, Disney and Universal basically give you the reins. As a theme park leader, you come to think nothing of managing a team of hundreds, or coordinating talent for the entire park, designed to serve and provide entertainment to the tens of thousands of guests who walk through the front gate on any given day. If you work in food and beverage, attractions, or operations, your management reach is similar. Whether you are in parks or resorts, onstage or backstage, you're managing people, situations, and systems. You must remain up to date on everything from contracts to procedures. You are placed in charge, with the full faith of the park execs, of millions of dollars of equipment. As a salaried leader, relationships are the key to getting everything done.

I recall a conversation I had with one of my former cast members, Angela, who moved to Nashville to become a front of house manager with a large resort. One of the questions posed to her was how she would manage an overwhelming crush of people. When she asked for clarification, the interviewer specifically talked about when people check in. The interviewer said she might only have one or two people at the front desk and three dozen families coming in during the same window of time. She told me she smiled at the recruiter and said, "In my position at the front of the park, I see that many people in a couple of minutes." She told me the interviewer raised her eyebrows. Angela said she continued by explaining that regardless of where you are in a Disney operation, you are part of an economy of scale where everybody is empowered to make the right decisions at any given time. That applies whether you are assisting one person or one hundred. If you're wondering whether she got the job, the answer is yes and no. You see, Angela applied for a guest service position. When they discovered her background and depth of experience, they offered her a role in management…which she accepted.

I personally never considered the scope and scale of the operations I managed until an executive pointed it out to me. He reminded me we have a daily staff of several hundred, and each one of those on-stage cast members interact with several thousand guests a day. There is a labor and cost center, as well as equipment operations, to oversee. The total material costs goes into the millions. Failing all those people comes at a price that is incomprehensible. That is why it cannot be allowed to happen. Teamwork allows the ship to move in a desired direction. We all work together, so it is crucial to have leaders who know the way.

To this day, I still make an effort to have conversations where I provide insight and feedback to those seeking it. On one of the podcasts I've done, I spoke about how theme park leadership is as different from leadership at other companies as cast and team members are from roles at other employers. In many cases, sometimes it's only the title that's different. In food and beverage, you will find managers touching tables, cleaning, running food, assisting in the kitchen, and greeting guests. You might find them at the front of the restaurant providing directions to a particular attraction or show. In attractions operations, you will find them in the greeter position, helping to load a venue, spieling, sweeping up a mess, and doing what needs to be done. Many of the managers who came through LMA got seat time, so they could understand what it was like to be in the cockpit of our show vehicles. They would also shadow techs to understand the technical ballet that took place backstage while the show was happening onstage. This was a key safety piece and eye-opening to new managers, where they discovered they could get mowed over by a car if they were not paying attention backstage during a show. The cars moved as fast backstage as they did onstage, because show timing demanded it.

Just like cast members, managers, and leaders in many Disney operations either have the background or the experience associated with that specific operation. In every new location, you learn about yourself and what you're capable of. At Disney and Universal, many of the managers and stage managers come from entertainment, so they understand the dynamics of the stage even if they've never been in a booth calling cues for a show. I have also worked with plenty of managers who had a limited entertainment background. One of our stage managers at "Wild Wild West" worked in characters briefly before moving over to conventions. His training period was similar in some ways to ours. He started by watching the show and then got a tour of the stage. After that, he was in the booth observing how the cue-to-cues worked. In almost every show where I've called cues, I worked with techs who knew the shows better than I did. There were some occasions where I would have a tech who knew the equipment but not the show. It is critically important to make sure every cue is fired on time. Like the speeding cars and motorcycles, sometimes, what's happening backstage can be just as exciting as what's happening onstage.

Disney taught me a great deal about myself as a person and leader. It taught me that I wanted to become a Disney leader by title, because the official title came with greater responsibility and access. I realized if I could reach people one class at a time at the Traditions level, how much greater would my reach be as an operations manager? How many more could I motivate and inspire? As it turns out, a whole bunch (which is an actual scale of measurement). Disney gave me the platform to develop my servant leadership mindset. I knew very little about this process beforehand. Observing leaders in positions I aspired towards allowed me to borrow the traits I admired most in them as I found my own footing. Researching Robert Greenleaf and the mindset that launched servant leadership helped cement my own intentional focus. But before all that, I needed to figure out what existed beyond the walls of LMA.

My own leader and proprietor at LMA supported this foray by setting up shadow opportunities along with meet and greets. With the shadow opportunities, I had the chance to spend the day with managers in attractions operations, which I was already somewhat familiar with. I also spent time at food and beverage, resorts, and recreation. My last shadow was with Disney Photo Imaging. I later learned that the proprietor of DPI was evaluating me as much as I was evaluating their operation. When I went through my first Leadership Casting Call (LCC), I discovered this leader of leaders wanted to know everything about me that he could. After he brought me onto his team, I hit the ground running. He allowed me to learn, stumble, and grow. That is the kind of leader everyone deserves. Just in case you aren't sure, stumbling is necessary. Failures allow us to clock our learning curve. People working with you, especially those seasoned managers, can offer valuable insights as you develop your relationships with them.

To every end, building relationships is important beyond the ways you might imagine. One day backstage at LMA, Lloyd walked into the green room. After I said hi, I pointed to his name tag and said, "You know, Lloyd, costuming will replace that for free because right now it doesn't look like Good Show." The face of his name tag looked like he had been asphalt surfing on it. It was scratched and scraped up, a great example of Bad Show. Bear in mind, when I said this, I was a stunt driver - an hourly cast member - and he was my manager's manager. But he nodded and said I was right.

Lloyd later told me he used this experience in the leadership casting call, the LCC. When they asked me to leave the room so they could discuss my merits and debate whether or not to move me up to the management bench, their biggest concern was if I could hold others accountable. Lloyd shared this story, relating how unflinchingly I encouraged a senior leader towards the standards that applied to everyone else. This example was good enough for the interview committee, and they moved me to the next series of interviews.

I advise anyone who falls into a leadership position, by intention or by promotion, to get on their own leader's calendar as quickly as possible. From my personal experience, I can share the following: some leaders will want you to get a feel for the area and understand the lay of the land. Sometimes you will shadow a seasoned manager so as to become intimately acquainted with the various nuanced aspects of the business itself. Sometimes your leader will give you one thing to be responsible for and you are not, under any circumstances, to deviate from that one thing. Sometimes your leadership will change, and you will have to learn what your new leader wants, values, and finds important. Be quick to ask questions and take notes. Move slowly to affect change. Frequently, things that don't make sense starting out begin to make sense after you've been in the operation for a while. Sometimes, a way of doing things may not seem ideal but serves everyone best. If you have the luxury of time, spend the first six to twelve weeks taking notes before looking to initiate changes.

As a newly minted manager, I knew I was occasionally a pain in the butt for my proprietor, but by his own confession, he wouldn't have had it any other way. The way I looked at things and my passion for Disney's legacy appealed to him. He (mostly) appreciated that I had no filter when it came to asking questions about how things were done, or what could be done to change things, should a better way be discovered. But at times, I didn't know when to let something go. If someone on your team has been around or on that team for far longer than you and gently suggests you drop a pursuit, it never hurts to ask their insights as to why before continuing. I'm not bragging about being the occasional pain in the neck. My priority was making sure our frontline cast members were being taken care of. That they knew we were constantly looking out for them was of key importance to me. As I grew into a more experienced manager, I learned that if my people knew I was lobbying on their behalf, speaking up as their voice and advocate, they would be willing to come through for me, and the operation, as well.

So, here we are. You are entertaining the idea of leaving the comfort of Disney or Universal, or you have already left. What's next and how do you get there?

Many people who leave a theme park operation don't have a fully fleshed out plan in place. People who leave jobs do so one of two ways. In the first way, they leave to go to another company. Either they seek the position out, or this company headhunts them. Once they know they're going to be brought on board somewhere else, they tender their notice at their current job. In the second way, people leave a role because they don't want to stay in the operation anymore and they're willing to take their chances, or they believe their best chance at succeeding with their side gig won't happen until they give it their full attention. It goes to the point of people leaving people, and not companies, but that is a section unto itself.

There are a few people I know, including an actor friend I've doubled, who knew he was going to change over from contracted to sub when the opportunity appeared on his radar. In his case, he had been booking so much film and TV work that he felt bad having others cover his shifts so often. He realized that if he gave up his contract, it gave another actor an opportunity. He eventually moved to Hollywood, came back to Orlando

a few times a year to pick up shifts, then finally decided
to stay put on the West Coast. I saw him not too long ago
when we worked together on a project in Atlanta. His
reach now extends into directing and producing, as well
as teaching master classes on acting. When we met up,
he talked about one of his directing projects that had just
premiered. He understood exactly when it was time to
leave Disney. He had been spending more time focused
on work he booked, work he was auditioning for, and
other projects. Having to coordinate time to schedule
flights, a place to stay, and shifts was becoming an
onerous logistical burden. It made more sense for him to
simply leave the company entirely. He told me he knew
it was time to go, and to trust that others would be
making magic in his absence. Where had I heard that
before?

Another person who immediately comes to mind
gave up his contract because he was building a business.
Over the course of three years, he went from a full-time
to a part-time contract, and then finally realized he had
to be all in with his business. He confessed that it was
one of the hardest and scariest decisions he had made in
a long time. He had one child with another on the way,
and he was walking away from the known, sure thing - a
steady paycheck - into the unknown. He was trading in
his velvet handcuffs for the freedom of the unknown. In
the entertainment and theatrical world, he was a
powerful, known entity. He had done several national
tours before deciding to call Orlando and Disney home. I
understood completely. When I made my commitment to
film and TV as a career, I had no Plan B. I had to do it
for the same reason that I write: I could not imagine not

doing it. When he made the decision to leave Disney, it was because he wanted to go all in on something else, and he told me going all in ultimately allowed him to be wildly successful as a musical theater performer.

Another gentleman who started in theme park operations as a character performer worked his way up the promotional ladder to become an executive responsible for key components of the Orlando operation. He made the choice to leave because he wanted to build his consulting business, he was working on a book, and after a lengthy talk with his wife, he knew the correct decision was the one where he handed over his theme park ID, keys, and vehicle. That's right. He was high enough on the food chain that he had his own company vehicle, a nice perk. But when it is time to leave, it is time to leave. The smart ones know because they feel it.

Many people who leave Disney when they are in managerial or entertainment positions are frequently courted by another company. The individual usually takes advantage of these other opportunities because it's clearly a vertical movement for them. But what if this isn't the case for you? What if operational downsizing or restructuring means you now no longer having a role to show up for every day? Just as it happens in the corporate landscape, it happens in theme parks. It can happen because the position is seasonal, and it can happen because there has been an organizational shift. It can happen because of good old fashion politics. Regardless, if you find yourself in this position, this won't adversely impact your ability to walk through the next door. This applies across the board, no matter your position and no matter the company. But I'm going to say something that might very well be considered taboo or blasphemy: getting fired, terminated, or released from a position, job or company is not the scarlet letter that will forever prevent you from working for any other organization, or starting your own business in the future. These things happen, and people understand.

The following is going to be one of the most unconventional pieces of advice anyone in a post-job-loss or departure-job-hunt is ever going to hear, but here it is: take a week or two to work through your thoughts, feelings, and get your bearings. If you need time, and your finances allow it, take a month. During this period, grab a sheet of paper, your computer, or your phone and create a list of things you've done as well as a list of things you can do. Think about the things you want to do. Figure out how all these come together into a Venn diagram. Identify how they connect. That is the field where your strengths play. It's also a great time to noodle with your résumé or CV, even write a cover letter. In conjunction with this activity, reach out to the confidantes in your circle.

Early in my film and TV career, I was given a great piece of advice. A friend in the business with several decades of experience told me that after every audition - regardless of whether she thinks she booked it - she plans an activity for herself. It could be a movie, maybe it's visiting with some friends, maybe it's a trip to a favorite restaurant or watering hole with a great view. She does this because the distraction keeps her from getting in her own head. I acted on her advice and found it wildly beneficial. If you choose to do the same, make sure your distraction is something positive. I found doing so helps awaken a different part of my mind, the creative piece that works through logic differently. Your mind is problem-solving creatively and at hyper-speed. Our best discoveries happen precisely when we are not looking for them.

Once you have an idea of what you're looking for in the next steps of your career, figure out what you need to get there. Do you need a headhunter? Is there a friend connected to a place or business you'd like to be part of? There is oftentimes more than one way to get where you're going.

Right around the time my mom and dad decided to move to North Carolina, dad had a conference happening in Asheville. He wound up meeting an old friend for lunch. They both worked together at the same company in South Florida years prior. They didn't talk about business until dad mentioned he and mom were moving up there. He wanted to know what the commercial restaurant space looked like from a business and job market perspective. His buddy told my dad if he needed or wanted a job when he got up there, he had one waiting.

Sometimes it's as simple as putting your information out into the cybersphere. Platforms like LinkedIn can be ideal for connecting with people you've worked with and individuals who are hiring, looking for someone with your skill set.

Another thing to add to the list you created? Two more columns. One highlighting all the things that brought you joy and the opportunities that came about because of them. The second column is for the frustrations you felt were insurmountable. For me, there were a few, but they were well beyond my reach. Once I understood certain things were beyond my control, I learned to let those things go. Hanging on to such issues only interferes with your ability to produce the energy and effort you are compelled to deliver. Energy doesn't know what to do until we assign it a value. I found I got more accomplished by giving my energy a positive direction. You get more bees with honey than you do with vinegar.

There's a simple reason you want to identify frustrations which may have interfered with your ability to perform; you might come across similar challenges in new work environments. I compare it to camping. When you're primitive or tent-camping, the first thing you do is find a flat area, and then you clear it of rocks, branches, and debris. If you do not, when you fall asleep, even the smallest pebble under your shoulder blade feels like a jabbing boulder. The small things are amplified, and they can become triggers and roadblocks. It is always best to do everything you can either to mitigate or avoid such issues up front. Another reason to identify these frustrations is because it gives you the opportunity to figure out what caused them to be troublesome, and what solutions might have mitigated the stress they brought you. How you've addressed a challenge in a work setting is a popular interview question. Giving a good, knowledgeable, and reflective answer goes a long way to shoring up support from the interviewer, necessary especially if the interview is part of a multi-stage process.

In the months following the pandemic, when companies started hiring again, some of them put new safety protocols in place. Others were creating a remote or hybrid work structure. I marveled at the connective fabric the social media platform LinkedIn provided for these people and businesses. Individuals I worked with at Disney were landing positions in other companies, and in many cases gesturing for others to follow. Others decided to put wheels on an idea that was inch-worming through their brains. Some of these individuals were former Disney cooks, others were Disney carpenters, some were Disney writers, and others were applying their passion for mentoring and consulting by simply making themselves available. For many of these people, their new idea became their new direction.

A friend of mine who worked as a Disney chef for many years started cooking for people after the pandemic, when he began traveling again. He loves travel, and loves cooking and preparing dishes that tell the taste buds a story. He would do eight to ten plus serving options, all with a flavor profile or theme like Barbecue, Polynesian, Mediterranean, African, and your basic American cuisine. He became so busy he had to hire an assistant, and then another. When he got the call to come back to Disney, he turned them down. He was so busy, booked several weeks out, that he couldn't imagine calling off his new passion. He created tasting menus and partnered with other chefs, going so far as to do a regional tour where he rented beautiful mansions and homes, selling tickets to the experience. He provided for the food lover an experience unlike any other. He donates a portion of the proceeds from these events to charity and continues to be very much in demand.

It was remarkable to hear him say almost verbatim what I felt: he confessed he never saw himself leaving Disney, let alone saying no to them when they asked him to come back. But his opportunities and ability had outgrown his previous station. Now, he has people besides just his family depending on him, and he was happy to be on this new journey.

We both readily agreed we loved Disney and were thankful for each opportunity that came our way. When you focus on your time at Disney or Universal, think about where you were when you started and where you were when you left. There's a tremendous chance you have grown as a person, and your skill set has kept pace with that growth, or even leap-frogged to a place you hadn't previously imagined possible. Even if you started and ended in the same position, you have still grown thanks to training, experience, and the contingencies you encountered.

Another friend, Meg, converted her knowledge of Disney parks and resorts into self-guided, interactive tours. She provides activities for the kids in the family and projects the entire family can do together. For research, she and her husband, along with their kids, go to stay at resorts and experience everything just as a guest would, then she adds her own knowledge to create one-of-a-kind products and experiences. She has built such a following that she's started creating merchandise.

When we spoke, she told me she has branched out to include the Universal parks in her offerings. Her long range plans focus on not only theme parks in the Central Florida corridor, but other destinations throughout the country. She's creating a ribbon or medal for when people accomplish a certain series of tours and constantly looking for ways to enhance the experience. Meg created this wonderful opportunity for herself and others from her knowledge, passion, and experience working at a theme park. Once you learn how to make pixie dust, you can do it anywhere. That's because theme park training teaches one to think and reach beyond their immediate vicinity. Where you show up for your day is only a starting point for what you will have the ability to do, both for yourself and others.

In all of these cases, nobody is spilling the beans on proprietary or confidential information. They are simply sharing their own perspective and experience, "plussing" it in their own way. Like Walt Disney, who would readily admit he didn't invent the theme park - he just saw an opportunity to enhance an existing concept - these people have taken their theme park background and leveraged it for the benefit of the far-flung communities they now serve.

I am still very much a theme park advocate. Under the parks and resort umbrella, there is no shortage of opportunities and roles or positions in their number and diversity. White collar, blue collar, entertainment, food, and beverage, administrative, legal, marketing, and thousands more. Thousands. When I was a cast member and a team member, I was an unofficial ambassador for the respective organization, and I am still that way. I cannot help myself. When people are talking about their first trip to Disney, I find myself weighing in once I learn where they're going and what they want to do. I have continued to share my knowledge through public speaking engagements, podcasts, writing, and the ever-present one-on-one conversations, which I believe is going to be a constant for the rest of my life. And you know what? I am totally fine with that. Disney was a dream for me. Six Flags taught me it was all in a day's work to wear multiple hats, but the reward was a tenfold return in opportunities. Universal was my launchpad for live shows and stunts. These companies with their theme park and resort operations have established a standard by which I, for good or bad, measure other companies and organizations.

If these vast global entertainment giants can maintain the same standards of performance excellence while carefully protecting their brands and ensuring the best possible experience, there's no excuse for smaller companies not to do the same. Excellent guest service costs nothing extra.

No matter your position at a theme park or resort operation, even after you leave, your perspective for service excellence remains with you for life. It becomes a filter by which you measure all others. It's a standard that you will hold yourself to unwittingly, no matter what your next objective is. With Disney, anybody who ever scoffed at the statement, "Once a Cast Member, always a Cast Member," need only watch somebody give directions. You will invariably see that classic two-finger point. If someone is providing directions with the assistance of a map, they might adjust the map and orient it against where they are standing. I still turn a map on its side and begin listing landmarks whenever someone asks me for directions. It is important for me to be able to help others, and has always been the case in every position I ever held. It is a mindset that remains with me to this day. You get it, especially if you are nodding your head, because you've been there, too, and you are. Likewise motivated. It sounds simple, but there is never anything wrong with making the world a better place by starting with the space that surrounds us.

Building Your Résumé or CV

It's important to make your résumé stand out; ensuring that it's easy to navigate is just as important. There are countless studies that talk about the limited number of seconds one has to get someone's attention, digitally and on paper. We have all developed a shorter attention span, and whether intentionally or not, we quickly work to assess, label, and compartmentalize new information. It's only when we focus on mono or hyper-tasking that we give every single thing the attention it deserves. For better or worse, the average HR individual spends less than seven seconds looking at your résumé. Here are a few things to consider when creating or updating your CV. This is a starting point, and it applies anywhere you go, including if you find yourself called back to the theme park where it all started for you.

Lominger Competencies.

If you're not familiar with this term, get yourselves acquainted and see which of the competencies apply to the roles you filled while with The Walt Disney Company, Universal, or whatever entertainment and tourism destination of which you were a part. There are two reasons why you want to include these competencies on your résumé.

1) Meta-data searches. Increasingly, the first set of eyes that see your résumé or CV is a digital, optical, AI-enhanced eye. It's designed to look for specific words, frequencies, and how they are applied. The right words will get you the right kind of attention and an actual human to follow up. This process of initial weeding out is not going to change. With the sheer volume of submissions some companies get for positions, it's the only way they can provide the appropriate attention to the right candidates.

2) What the hiring department is looking for. On my résumé, you will find things such as Compassion, Managing Diversity, Critical Thinking, Action Oriented, and Creative Thinking. These are some of the things I have applied in one or more of my roles at just about any theme park position. Moving around from position to position might seem strange to someone not familiar with the way theme park training and job placement works, but your skills are just as transferable as the terminology used to describe them is relatable. Plugging these words in as stand-alones, in one or two columns, creates easily consumable, bite-sized nuggets of important information for a recruiter.

Here is an example of what these competencies look like when appearing on a résumé:

EXPERIENCED MANAGER & TRAINER of PROJECTS & TEAMS

Action-oriented, unifying leader with over 30 years in film, live show and theme park entertainment. High performer on projects & teams; Builds and drives through integrity, trust and organizational agility. Committed to personal development, mentorship and a work/life balance. Brings partnership, perspective and a strategy mindset to every project.

- Creative & Innovative Management • Motivating Others
- Written/Verbal Communication • Managing Diversity
- LeadershipPresentation Skills • Action Oriented • Creative Thinking
- Caring for Direct Reports • Adherence to Proprietary Protocols

What appears in the above section is not comprehensive (there are sixty-seven Lominger competencies). This is my preferred way to feature these competencies, but is not the only way. You may decide to feature a few in short-form sentences, for example. Do the research so you know which ones apply to you personally. Know these competencies and identify the ones that apply to the theme park roles you held. This will help the recruiter understand your past work and future capabilities even better. A recruiter's time is at a premium. If you get on their schedule because of your résumé, be prepared to take advantage of that. Contrary to popular belief, the interview process is a two-way street and not a place to be passive. This kind of engagement is critical to capturing the attention of the interviewer, which is key to putting you in the driver's seat as far as position placement.

Résumé Format.

Everyone has an opinion on the matter, and mine is simple: do the research, and you will find plenty of up-to-date, easy to navigate templates. You want to be current, format-wise, as far as what hiring operations and employers are looking for. Some aspects of résumé writing remain timeless, like short bullet points. This is a given, but your contact info should also be easy to find. If you're having to manage your expenses, fear not; most of these templates are free. Another good free resource? Just about any online video platform. In fact, if you use your favorite search engine and enter the words "résumé template", you'll find plenty of options. At this point, just check the date of posting and look at a few different posts to get a well-rounded idea of what employers currently look for. Depending on the industry, the résumé or CV formatting will differ from position to position.

If you are taking classes of any kind, you probably have access to the associated educational institution's library and staff. Most universities have a career center where résumé services are provided for free. Many organizations provide access to companies that do résumé assessments and formatting. Some may also provide access to headhunting organizations. At Disney, this service proved to be so popular and so successful that they have continued this post-employment process with no sunset on its availability.

Find out what assets are out there for you to utilize. Key among them are the people you know. Just as there is someone who likely has a contact at a company you're interested in, I guarantee there's someone in your direct circle who knows how to format a résumé for optimal attention and mileage. Bottom line, people pay attention when they notice that you pay attention to details. It applies at Disney, it applies at Universal, and it applies elsewhere in the world.

Interviews: Staging

Now that you've updated your résumé, you reached out to former peers, you put the word out, and you have interviews coming up. Huzzah and congratulations! As in acting, sometimes the hardest part of a role is getting asked to audition. But you got the audition, or the interview, and that is a noteworthy first step.

If your interview is over the phone, make sure you are somewhere quiet, with privacy, as you'll likely you need it. You don't want distractions, and you don't want the person on the other end of the call to have those distractions either. Unnecessary background noice can torpedo your interview before it starts. If the interview is a video format, the same considerations apply., but you also have to visually present as professional. Be aware of your lighting. I recommend investing in a small four-to-ten-inch ring light (they do a great job of lighting you up). If you cannot get a ring light or do not have one, use a two-lamp set up where the lights are at 45 degree angles to the front of your face, not too bright, and limited shadows. When considering your background, be intentional and careful how you stage. Perhaps you have a place in your bedroom close to a corner. Grab a chair, grab a folding table or anything else that will work, and set up. Experiment with the lighting and background well before the interview itself. Trying to get everything ready fifteen minutes beforehand will only stress you out, whereas thirty minutes will give you the time you need to set up, power up, and make sure you're professional mindset wise, and camera ready.

Optics. If you're not exactly sure what the camera sees, even when you're looking at it, point your phone at the background you intend to use and take a picture. Plain is perfect, but you can also have a few things behind you that reflect your personality and passion, as long as they are appropriate. If, after studying the backdrop for your interview, nothing glaring grabs your attention, then you've hit the ideal.

If your living environment does not afford you the ability to create and stage a space for the interview, conduct it outside. Find a park, or even some plants and shrubs near where you live and use them as your backdrop. If you are close to your home, you can conduct the interview outside with easy access to your own Wi-Fi signal. Get a small ring camera that clips to the top of your computer or phone. Grab a folding chair or a camp chair. Dress appropriately. Interviewers understand, and just like with an audition, they want you to do well. One thing to consider is your virtual background. Some companies do not care, and others do. Make that choice but be ready to switch it off if you are asked to. Your real background should never be that four-and-a-half-week pile of dirty laundry or beer can on the nightstand. Should you have to conduct the interview from your bedroom, if at all possible, set up the camera or computer with a background that does not include your bed. I have a friend who has several video conferences every week. Sometimes these happen with individuals in time zones halfway around the world. She'll set the computer up on a laptop hard surface pillow, on her bed, and she will sit on a folding chair in front of it. She has a couple of 3M hooks that she hangs pictures from. If you are ever on a video call with her, you would have no idea. It's tremendously convenient, especially when she has one of these in the middle of the night. It looks professional, and that is what matters. Make certain your device is fully charged. If you have to scrounge for an outlet midway through, you'll only look disorganized and unprofessional. Whatever you do, I cannot reiterate this enough: no distractions. Also, no alcohol (I have to say this because somebody has done it).

When you are traveling and you know you have a video appointment or video content to produce, study your surroundings so that you can lock down a location. I have conducted video appointments, interviews, and featured speeches in a wide variety of environments, everything from my bedroom to the beach, from hotel lobbies to hotel rooms. In every case, the space presented professionally, or at the very least, cleanly. It is easy to accomplish and just takes a little time and effort.

If you're not traveling without a separate mic, here's a helpful audio trick for you: grab a towel and drape it around (but not over) the device mic. This works on computers, tablets, and phones. The material will soften the edge in your voice and minimize the echo created by hard surfaces. Your computer should have a resident audio monitor. Use it to figure out how loud you sound and how close you need to be to the device for optimal audio. On a tablet or phone, use the dictation or voice recording feature to see how you sound. Even if this sounds like an awful lot of work for an interview, it all goes back to the original philosophy: details matter. As the interviewee, you want to be at least as professional as the interviewer. I promise, all this only takes a few extra minutes but pays off enormously.

Why is staging important? Why is the removal of distractions important? Why is making sure your audio controls are top notch so important? Because you want to be able to make your message land, and you want it to be sticky. If you go to the movies and people are talking, or opening cellophane-wrapped candy, it takes you out of the show. If the sound system in the theatre is in poor shape, you will not enjoy the theatre experience. You never want to distract from your professional image. Interviewers are talking to dozens of people every day, in a host of different environments. You want to stand out for all the right reasons. Staging is important for the interviewer because they are assessing and grading the moment the connection is established. The interviewer may also be evaluating you based on what they see behind or around you. If you're interviewing for a position that calls for a high level of attention to detail, lack of attention to your surroundings will stand out, but not in the right way.

I once had a podcast interview scheduled while housesitting for a friend. I asked my friend if I could use his office - especially because I needed a door I could temporarily close between me and their two dogs. Once there, I grabbed an office chair and a barstool. I clipped my ring light to the camera while experimenting with the mic and acoustics in this new space. I made sure everything was good to go before the interview, because I not only needed to make sure that I presented well, but that there were no distractions for the viewers.

On another occasion, I was doing a digital leadership conference, where each of us contributed thirteen to fifteen-minute live segments available to any participants tuning in. I was traveling at the time, so I did not have access to my home studio. Instead, I was in a rather ordinary looking hotel room. I looked around and decided to use the back wall, where the TV was. I pulled the desk away from the wall and set it up in the center of the room. I moved one of the torch lamps to the end of the dresser where the TV stood. I pulled a Mickey Mouse, Kermit, and Eeyore plush out of my vehicle and posed them up against the TV, like they were also staring into the camera. I framed the camera, so the critters hovered just over my shoulder. I did all this in the morning, so all I had to do before the interview itself was shower, shave, and find my spotlight. I have a colleague who uses a mic, backdrop, and stanchion system both at home and when he travels. He said that no matter where he is, he can always control what's behind him, and because he uses a ring light system, his lighting is always exactly the same. Another colleague travels with a green screen, and because he is frequently globetrotting, he will capture images or video of the town where he is. He'll have one of these appear on his green screen background. He prefers it to a generated background because there aren't the normal distracting border issues. In both cases, I love the idea of the consistency here. For you, it only needs to be as simple as having a background that does not distract. That background can be fun and it can tell a little about who you are. If you'd rather, it can be all business. Just make sure it is intentional, and not a disaster.

Interviews: Talking the Talk

On the day of the interview, all the usual bits of advice apply. Make sure you are well-rested, make sure you are dressed appropriately, and make sure you are 100% attentive. Have a thermos, water bottle, mug, or glass with water nearby. It doesn't hurt to have a few cough drops on hand as well, just in case. Nothing is more frustrating than an uncontrollable cough, and you can count on a throat tickle exactly when you don't want one. Better to be proactive.

As mentioned before, working for Disney or Universal can entail being shuttled from position to position in a way that is unique from other corporate work environments. Most companies don't have three thousand job classifications. Most organizations don't offer the opportunity to move between differing lines of business with the ease companies like Universal and Disney do. When someone wants to know why you didn't seem capable of holding onto a job for longer than six months to a year, take the opportunity to explain the theme park way of learning, training, leading, and gaining experience. This is why it is critical you be prepared to talk about how Disney and Universal hires and provides opportunities to its employees. It wasn't that you couldn't keep a position; it was that you took advantage of opportunities presented. Most individuals in other people resource operations have no idea how staffing works in the theme park and resort world. You get to fill them in when you're sitting down for that interview. Not only do you get to share with and educate them, but you pave the way for the former theme park employees who follow in your footsteps. It is said when someone gets their private pilot license, that this is a license to learn. It almost feels the exact same way when one gets hired at either Disney or Universal. Your first role is your starting point.

During the interview, Show your enthusiasm. Punctuate with stories and examples. I discussed earlier how, in an audition, the people on the other side of the table want you to do well. They want you to be right for the part. They want you to hit it out of the park. They may have already mentally plugged you into a role or position. In an interview, it's no different. Give the interviewer the best and most honest version of yourself that you can. Even if you discover throughout the process that a particular position isn't for you, try to rise to the top anyway. In this era of ongoing conglomerations, affiliations, and mergers, the company might have another line of business within a larger organization that falls within your wheelhouse. Leaving a wonderful impression is a surefire way of getting additional consideration. When asked, talk about awards or recognition you may have received, and do so in a way that focuses on the people, actions and projects that got you there. You did something significant to be recognized, so dig into those experiences, using measurable metrics that people outside of the theme part industry can understand. Whenever possible, make clear you could not and did not accomplish or achieve without the partnership of others.

When I created the Disney University tour "From Motors to Action: Launching an Explosive Show", I became a de-facto expert of the stage regarding its history and safety procedures. General research, meetings with Imagineers and conversations with show runners from the original Paris show gave me source material by which to build the tour, while having access to a plethora of quick facts and trivia to share. I wanted to make sure people walked away from the show with so much information to be enthusiastic about that they would have no choice but to share it. The tour was designed to entertain and educate. Facts tell and stories sell. I did both. I wanted people to have fun above and beyond the fact they were walking on the actual set. For example, upon learning that the LMA village was based architecturally on the town of Villefranche-Sur-Mer, I shared photos of the village that inspired and brought our set to life. I leveraged contacts who had contacts. One of the techs was friends with an Imagineer who worked on the original portfolio for the Paris show. He got me a "making of" DVD that showed not only behind-the-scenes footage of the show's creation, but also featured interviews with Stunt Coordinator Rémy Julienne, the creative force behind the show and its electrifying stunts.

Incidentally, it's no accident that the show has a strong spy and espionage angle to it. Among the many credits for second unit work and stunts he has done, Rémy worked on several James Bond films. Actually, the stunt show was *supposed* to be James Bond themed, but the Disney creative team was unable to negotiate that outcome with the Broccoli estate. Even though they couldn't secure the character, Disney proceeded ahead with the genre. The creative team correctly predicted it would still play well for audiences. The show and its theme of intrigue, layered onto a series of consecutively more and more dangerous stunts, played very well indeed. The original show, "Moteurs, Action!" ran for eighteen years, while "Lights Motors Action" played for eleven.

Through this research, I discovered that LMA had the best safety record of any stunt show in the world. As a result, I became one of the show's go-to safety experts.

Being able to talk at length about the *why* and *how* behind the show's safety procedures proved to be a transferable skill that, in time, would have me giving presentations not only to Disney Cast Members, but also to airline executives, tech industry specialists, and Disney Institute participants, all interested in incorporating some part of the Disney way into their own companies.

When my career search led me beyond the realm of Disney's kingdom, I shared with anyone who would listen my experience creating the Disney University tour. Any opportunity was a relevant opportunity. It highlighted my ability to create content, build relationships individually and inter-departmentally, and navigate the various steps it takes to produce a finished product within an entertainment company the size of Disney. Do the same for any such things you have participated in or created during your time working for a theme park. You don't have to build tours to showcase impressive work. Anything you have done to make a difference is a way in which you can showcase your skillsets and accomplishments. Anything you have accomplished likely happened as a result of partnerships. Always remember to talk about partnerships, because working with others is a skill set onto itself, and one many hiring agents are looking for.

Why is all of this important? Nothing in my job description when I got hired to the stunt show said "tour guide" or "subject matter expert for safety protocols". Nothing in the title said "activity coordinator" or "guy uniquely trained and qualified to extinguish the flames of a person fully engulfed in fire". I picked up these responsibilities over time by asking two questions. First, "What can I do to make a difference?" Second, simply, "What about this?" Sometimes I'd simply say, "Train for something new? You bet!"

Never get deterred by a "no" or "not right now". Every idea and concept or project you pitch that gets a no is one that is getting you a step closer to a yes. Quite a few of my ideas were met with shaking heads, but that didn't stop me from coming back with new ones.

During your interview, share your own take on making a difference. Believe it or not, it can have a tremendous impact on the outcome of the interview or conversation. Regardless of the theme park and regardless of the role, use your job title as a starting point, not the bookends. Every single position, no matter how generalized or specific, is a launching pad for additional opportunities to make a difference. While on the stage, I looked for opportunities that permitted me to apply my passions. At the end of the day, that's how things like the LMA tour got created.

Accolades are great coming from others. Talking about what got you a blue Legacy name tag is infinitely more impressive than the name tag itself. I know some people might argue that having the name tag speaks volumes. But there's something I liked to share with every cast member who congratulated me or shared that they hoped to live up to the standards of the Legacy name tag one day. I always told them to look at the back of the name tag pinned to their chest: it was blue. They were already wearing a blue name tag.

When you are talking about your accomplishments and recognitions, allow your passion to come through. Speak from a place of truth and honesty. Be matter of fact. And take it a step further: have fun. When we speak of our passions, the energy comes from our heart. People hear the truth in our words because they are infused with excitement. You feel it. If you aren't specifically asked about activities beyond the scope of your job, find ways to include some of that information. Maybe you work with an animal rescue. Maybe you are involved in CAST, or United Way, or Toys for Tots, or anything VoluntEAR related. Maybe you work with the local food banks, Habitat for Humanity, or the Make-A-Wish foundation. Personally, I'm proud of my Presidential service pins and my RunDisney-style VoluntEAR medallion. At Universal, we had an Adopt-A-Kid program. Around the holidays, we got empty backpacks delivered to our stage with a piece of paper attached to each, listing the child's name and a few things they wanted or needed. I don't think I ever had so much fun shopping. Making a difference comes in all shapes and sizes.

Remember, there are going to be varying degrees of what potential employers are looking to hear. Some only care that you worked for Disney. Others are more interested in your successes at the company than they are the places where you encountered struggle. Still others want to know more about how you navigated the challenges you encountered. The smart interviewers engage you in conversation and ask you scenario and solution-based questions. The smart candidate is prepared to answer, checking all the boxes in the process.

When I taught Traditions, I made sure I had pocket examples of things like the Four (now Five) Keys. Pocket examples are like elevator pitches. They allow you to draw from a single experience and explain its relevance no matter the scope of the question. These examples are tremendously important when you are asked scenario-based questions in an interview. Pocket examples are crucial when you are asked to give an opinion on a particular action or workplace philosophy.

At both Disney and Universal, I came to understand the way to tell a story changes based on the audience. Some need more details than others. Some want different details. Some do not care about the details at all. It's the sausage metaphor. Some want to see how the sausage is made, and others are more interested in how it looks on their plate. For some, it's watching the magic in all its splendor. For others, they need to see how the magic trick works. Some, believe it or not, want to know what happens when the magic doesn't work. Tailor your story and you enhance the connection. Double down on this when it comes to interviews and career movement opportunities.

You can also share a time that had nothing to do with your theme park experiences yet was a direct result of your training. Here is a personal example. I did a considerable amount of traveling last year (achieving and surpassing Medallion status with Delta, which was a *bunch* of miles). During one of my flights, I noticed the time of the connecting leg's departure kept getting extended, and I suspected this was because the airline was having a hard time finding a flight crew. Sure enough, a connecting flight that should've left ATL at 2:15 in the afternoon got pushed multiple times before finally being canceled at 11:25 p.m., 35 minutes before midnight. When I saw this happen on the overhead monitor, I walked to the customer service counter for the airline, which was already busy.

At the front of the line, I smiled and simply asked the gentleman behind the counter, "What can I do to make your life easier?" He smiled as I handed him my boarding pass. He scanned it and handed me a voucher for overnight accommodations and breakfast. He told me to enjoy my stay and that he put me in standby for the following day. The question I had asked, the one about how I could make that person's life easier? I've always believed asking that question is the best way to defuse a situation, no matter what side of the counter you are on. It's also a great way to open up additional opportunities. Waiting in line, I heard many people saying unkind things to the individuals behind the counter, as if the customer service agents were directly responsible for ruining travel plans (a sentiment I was intimately acquainted with when an irate parent would blame me for ruining their vacation at Disney because a particularly princess or character would not be appearing for any more except that day). There are plenty of things someone in a service position can do, but they also have the right to say no. In almost any theme park environment, the focus is always to solve for yes. If you approach the situation genuinely wanting to identify a solution, the individual across from you is more likely to go above and beyond for you.

Who hasn't been in a situation where the thing they're waiting for is delayed for reasons outside of their control, looking for someone to blame, and often taking it out on the first poor soul that crosses their path, wearing the right badge on their uniform? Sometimes, it's as simple as putting yourself in someone else's shoes.

Why not make it a rule to try and get more bees with honey than with vinegar? I've used this expression before for a reason. It is a thoughtful way of contemplating what your next move is going to be. We are all in this together, and the sooner people understand this, the better off we all are. You simply get more done when you start from a place of giving. More times than I will ever be able to count, I used this logic and process to help both guests and cast members. People know when you are genuinely trying to make a situation better. When that happens, they want to help with the outcome, a definite win-win situation for everyone involved. If you have an example of this sort of exchange, by all means, use it.

When talking about your theme park experience, do everything you can to focus on the positive. If you talk negatively about the operation, or the individuals in it, don't be surprised if you don't get the position. Why? Every single operation, every single role, job, and position has inherent responsibilities alongside inherited drama and friction. How we deal with the challenge of the challenge says more about our ability. Everyone can smile on a sunny day. What do you do when you're out in the rain without an umbrella? That is when others are paying attention.

Your interviewer may ask you *all* the questions. If there are certain questions you find difficult to answer, be delicate about how you handle them. Sometimes, in the case of challenges in the workplace, it's simply a matter of saying something along the lines of, "I recognized we had a difference of opinion but understood we were both committed to achieving the same goals." Learn to swerve and answer without tipping the interview against you. There's nothing wrong with steering an answer, as long as you are honest.

If it helps, think about it in some ways as if you're going on a date. You're at dinner, and the person you're sharing an appetizer with starts talking about their ex and doesn't stop until they've dug a hole deep enough to bury themselves and their ex under the mud. Their rhetoric is nothing but negative and acerbic. It's natural for you to wonder, "If this is how they talk about this person, will they talk about me in the same way one day?" With all the negative in the world, there's never too much positive to be had.

Your interview, whether it's the first or the third one, is still quite similar to a first date. Be honest, be yourself, be authentic, but don't be unpleasant, and don't throw mud. Even if you believe your criticism is justified, take the path of diplomacy. Speaking poorly of someone else in an interview, even if you think it's warranted, never speaks well for you. When asked if I ever worked for or reported to disagreeable managers, I always said that I learned to set my differences aside to serve the operation and those around me. If pressed, I usually said something along the lines of, "I believe they worked the best they could with the information and tools they had at the time." I also made it clear that sometimes, in my drive to accomplish things, I could be challenging to manage. This usually elicited follow-up questions, permitting me to explain I was able to reach a level of respect and understanding for every situation. I was very clear in explaining that over time I learned where it was appropriate to let the reins go and where it was appropriate to pull them in. No matter where you go in life, you are going to encounter challenges with people and situations. How you respond is how you move on.

It's okay to share your challenges, but always find a way to pivot towards the positive. Show how you managed to take a lemon and make enough lemonade to slake everyone's thirst. Use verbiage to demonstrate understanding that your perspectives or ideals did not align with a particular leader, but that did not prevent you from performing all the tasks you set out to accomplish on a given day.

We all end up at some point or other working with people we may not agree with, but we should never let that get in the way of what we want to get done. I once reported to a manager who didn't like the fact I was focused on building relationships with my hourly cast members. In the same breath she conceded that I knew more about the operation than she did because of those relationships. When you are the best, most honest version of you, people know what they are getting. During one of our one-on-one's, she asked why I spent time backstage and in the green rooms and break rooms. I told her that the cast members were my guests. If they knew I was checking in, and I was genuinely interested in their day, they would take care of the operation without fail. When your people take care of the operation because they feel the combination of trust, empowerment and a personal connection, the operation without fail takes care of the customers, and the customers take care of the bottom line.

When asked how I managed to turn what could have been a negative experience into a positive one (another good interview question to have a pocket example for), I share the story of a family I met outside the "Lights Motor Action" venue. We just finished our show, and I was heading out into the park to get a shot of pixie dust for myself in the shape of *One Man's Dream. One Man's*

Dream is a motivational experience for people who believe in the magic of Disney. It's the story of Walt Disney, his brother Roy, The Walt Disney Company, and its parks and resorts. The movie also talks of things yet to come, and much of it told in Walt's voice. Think *A Christmas Story*, or *It's A Wonderful Life*. One Man's Dream is the Disney version of story telling comfort food. It is truly educational and inspirational. I needed a bit of that inspiration. We'd had a particularly challenging warm-up and first show, so going to see *One Man's Dream* was my version of a walk in the park.

On the way out of the green room, I saw a family by the "Lights Motors Action" sign, announcing the time for the next two shows. Being who I am, I felt myself drawn to them. I found out they wanted to see Herbie, who was in our show. "They" was actually their little five-year-old boy, Christopher. I discovered they had to leave the park in less than an hour to catch a shuttle to the airport. I turned around, walked back into the green room, and went straight to the manager's office. I mentioned the family outside and asked if I could bring them around so their little boy could meet Herbie. The manager said yes even before I could finish asking. The importance of building relationships and having the respect of your leadership team cannot be overstated. They trusted me and my judgement to do what was right.

Unbeknownst to me, on my way out one of my friends, Paul, had overheard me and went to give Herbie a heads up. I got back to the family. I looked at the little boy and told him I had described him to Herbie, and Herbie had said, "Christopher? I've been waiting to see him all day!" The kid lit right up, the smile practically leaping from his face. I walked them through the queue and around the stage-left building façade. As we stepped onto the asphalt, Herbie appeared in one of the archways, rocking back-and-forth, his horn going off like nobody's business. Before anyone could react, Christopher broke into a run, scampering right up to Herbie. When he got to the magical Love Bug, he leaned forward and hugged the car's wheel well. Christopher's mom was in tears, his dad was filled with joy, and I just took it all in. We snapped some photos, and then I walked them out, happily on their way. Back in the green room, it occurred to me that my pixie rust had been converted to pixie dust just like that. I hugged Paul and thanked him for waking Herbie.

A letter came from the family, delivered to Guest Relations about three weeks later. Christopher said "Lights Motors Action" was his favorite show at Disney. They had been there less than five minutes - hadn't even gotten to see the show - but this is a great example of how transformative a magical moment can be. For me, this was a prime example of converting a loss to a win, of creating magic, of going above and beyond, and putting the needs of others ahead of my own. It's an example of doing what's right in the moment. I can't assign a value to the experience Christopher had with his mom and dad, but it's a safe bet he will never forget the day he met Herbie on the "Lights Motors Action" stage.

Think about your own theme park or resort experience. I'm confident there are similar narratives you've personally had a hand in, stories that you can share. The recruiter, the person in HR, your new manager, the people at your next mixer, they not only want to hear these stories, but they love to hear them. Sometimes it's because they have their own rich experiences, and other times it's because it is nothing more complicated than them wanting to learn more about you.

Many of us have directly or indirectly been involved in a critter adventure moment. That's where the family leaves the resort and a stuffed animal behind. Or, the family gets off the bus…and the Minion stays. And that's when the adventure begins. The lost stuffed animal makes it back home, along with photos or a photo album documenting their experience. This has happened in hospitals, airports, and museums. You don't need a license to create magic, just a desire.

Knowing what openings to listen for, you will be amazed at all the chances you have to share and engage during an interview. This is your chance to bring to life the experiences you lived and moments you had creating magic. It doesn't matter whether the market favors employees or employers, you have a built-in advantage coming from the ranks of either Universal Studios or Walt Disney Company. It's not limited to these two companies. Any hospitality operation or tourist destination provides its own set of transferable skills. Where some employees in hospitality-focused operations may deal with an influx of people during check-in or check out, if you come from a park operation, you dealt with the crush of humanity from park open to park close. Don't be shy when talking about these accomplishments and successes because such experience separates you from the pack.

When the time comes to leave the nest, when you deploy your wings to fly, you make room for the next cast member or team member to create happiness. It's okay and understandable to miss every part of the experience that brought you joy. It is okay to continue to talk in the present tense, as if you are still an employee of that theme park. There's a vested sense of ownership behind doing what we have done in park and resort operations. If you've ever been to a theme park and walked away with a smile on your face, more than likely it is because of the people working there. Sure, the rides, the food, and the shows help, but it's the name tag wearing battalion that are truly dedicated to creating happiness for you and yours while you're within the theme park gates.

Walt Disney said it best. "You can design and create and build the most wonderful place in the world. But it takes people to make the dream a reality." Humanity, singularly and collectively, is the first and finishing touch for every one of our core memories.

It is also perfectly reasonable if you discover, years later, that you're being drawn back by the tractor beams of Disney or Universal. Never say never. As I often told cast members leaving at the end of their College Program, "Go finish what you have to finish. Disney will still be here." So it goes for you and your next adventure. If you find yourself being contacted by talent casting, or a Disney casting recruiter, or a proprietor from an area you used to serve, take the time to listen to their offer. I have an old friend from my days at Florida Atlantic University who went on to get his master's and PhD. He then became a college professor. It was a great pay, great environment sort of experience. Yet he felt something was missing. That something was the sense of family. After a few years on the education hamster wheel, he knew he needed something familiar and different. He reached out to his old manager, and within a few months, he was back at Disney. He is probably one of the highest educated park ops cast members in the Magic Kingdom, but he couldn't be happier.

When I was doing the stunt show at Disney, one of our techs used to work backstage at Universal, so his was a friendly, familiar face I knew quite well. After about six months, he decided to put feelers out. As it turns out, one of his former Universal managers got in touch. The park was building a new show experience, and this manager wanted to know if he was interested in joining the team. He was having a great time at Disney but felt himself being pulled back to Universal, nonetheless.

Plenty of former cast members, team members, and DCL crew members become cast and crew members again, after completing their tour, contract, or whatever pulled them away. Going back to the theme park workspace is not like moving back in with your parents, but it is much like going home in other ways. There is a comfort and familiarity that will immediately bring joy not only to you, but to those you know.

Just as you brought skills with you when you left your role, you will surprise yourself with the transferable skill set you acquired while away. When I was teaching Disney Traditions, I was also afforded the opportunity to learn and deliver the content for Disney Cruise Line Traditions. When reviewing the roster, I'd discover people returning to DCL all the time. Some had moved on to boutique cruises, other to the big-name lines. Every single one of them said that the training for DCL was harder and the expectations were higher, but the opportunities on a Disney Cruise Line ship were also greater.

Take something from each of your experiences and see how they can be applied to whatever comes next. Whether the next chapter of your career adventure has you walking away from Universal or Disney, or walking back towards them, enjoy the adventure you are experiencing. Having worked in a theme park operation, you stand head and shoulders above those coming out of other industries. In many cases you represent the top 10% in a given line of business. No matter how long you stayed with Disney, Universal, or another theme park, regardless of whether it was in parks, resorts, or any other associated business, you proved that you have more than it takes.

When it came to leaving theme park employment, I learned a great deal by listening to other's experiences. Whether it was park operations, the Disney Cruise Line, food and beverage, or operation support, there are complementary legs of learning everywhere in the theme park industry. The stories, the podcasts, the conferences and keynote speeches? These in part made me realize people are interested in my experiences. The first time I was approached about doing a talk on leadership, I was a bit surprised, certain there were CEOs and C-suite executives who could speak ad nauseam on the topic. However, I learned that the way I approached managing in theme parks was of particular interest because I always stressed the collaborative nature of successful leadership. Teamwork makes the dreams work. That collaboration is in full force every time you tell a story, do an interview, or bring a project from creation to inception.

Think about how frequently people prod you to hear more about *you and your experience* when you tell them you work, or worked, in a theme park. They want to learn. Whether you were serving churros, performing five shows a day, dancing in a parade, or greeting people at the front of an attraction, you are a maker of magic; sharing a story or two only spreads that magic further. As far as others are concerned, you come from a place with the same complexity and color as the fabled land of Oz. If people are interested in my stories from the world of theme parks, I guarantee they are interested in yours. Learn how to tell those stories.

Never hesitate to share your stories, because they are as much a part of your adventure as the actions behind them.

Another thing. Never say never. Whether it is returning to theme parks or resorts, or returning back to where you started. It can feel final as you turn over your ID and walk out the doors. For many, it becomes more a matter of closing that chapter and writing a few more, before returning back to that book. I have been approached and I have interviewed with Disney several times since departing. For one reason or another, each one of those roles just wasn't quite the right fit for me. It doesn't mean I'm saying never. You should not, either.

I've known actors and other performers, stage managers, technicians, and people in engineering who left that world, convinced the theme park universe was in the rear view mirror. And for quite a few of those people, many of whom I am still friends with, I have often gotten a call with them beginning the conversation by saying, "Guess what? I'm going to Disney World, as a Cast Member!"

Sometimes, you may walk through the door and think you hear it being boarded up behind you. What you may actually be hearing is a better door being constructed for your future return. When it comes to any possibility of the positive, Never. Say. Never.

SO...YOU WANT TO HIRE A FORMER THEME PARK EMPLOYEE

Executives, HR professionals, recruiters and head hunters in any hiring department have a good idea of what they are looking for when they're hiring to fill positions. There are the usual qualifications of education, work experience, and technical proficiency (in today's world, even food servers are expected to be technically proficient to manage both static point-of-sale terminals and portable units). Every role, in one way or another, is going to expect you to know your way around a computer, even if an interaction is the simple depression of a few keys.

The interview process rarely starts with a paper application and a person to review it. Many companies, even smaller ones, employ online portals that use metadata searches. These systems use AI to sift through the unqualified and lesser qualified applicants. Even smaller companies leverage the services of third parties to manage and filter résumé submission processing. In these cases, the company might never actually see your application. While the upside for the organization is an automated process that allows initial qualifying to be done quickly and without costly human labor, on the downside these systems tend to exclude or fail to consider soft skills, with the exception of the Lominger Competencies mentioned earlier.

Take for example a former Disney employee, known as a cast member.

The hiring department of a particular hotel or resort might not consider hiring somebody that worked for a theme park, especially if their résumé has "Greeter", "Food and Beverage", or "Photographer" as their previous job title. It doesn't occur to hiring departments what skill sets and levels of expertise such individuals bring to the table, even when, in most cases, the people in these hiring departments have been to such parks as a guest. We always wear a different set of filters, or blinders, depending on what it is we want to see (consider the selective attention test of the Invisible Gorilla Experiment). When was the last time you went to a theme park, and it wasn't busy? Guests typically outnumber employees six to one. Yet with the models of efficiency introduced during training, these employees take care of a crowd's steady influx without batting an eyelash. Even when it is a comparatively quieter day in a theme park, certain elements like the show dump (the exodus from a theater when a show has ended) can look to the uninitiated like a flood of humanity released. That is because some of these theaters can hold thousands upon thousands of people.

These same hiring departments might balk at the idea of onboarding a former employee from another Disney operation such as a resort, Disney Vacation Club, Disney Cruise Line, or even a Disney Store. They might erroneously believe a former Disney employee might dilute the collective workforce skill set in their organization. I've heard people question exactly how difficult theme park work could possibly be. When compared to working at a hotel or food and beverage chain, it can be the difference between drinking from a garden hose and drinking from a dam flood gate. It's like comparing a leisurely bike ride with a BMX competition where the competitors are hurtling down the side of a mountain. Such beliefs shortchange both the potential of the applicant, the tool kit of tricks this potential new employee brings with them, and the growth metric potential within the hiring entity. Remember: most theme park orientation and initial on-the-job training is more complex and costs the company more in the first month post-onboarding than the average corporate employee will go through in the course of several years. Disney and Universal, for example, rely more on people than technology to do the training. They will continue to do so since people are the key to unlocking great experiences and memories. That potential new hire with a theme park background? Depending on the position within your company, thinking these individuals cannot contribute to whatever line of business you are hiring for is closing the door on a tremendous pool of highly qualified candidates.

Such beliefs do not have to be immovable. In a previous life, I was a financial advisor and broker. When I went to interview with Phil, the president of the firm, he was skeptical because I had no financial background outside of balancing a checkbook. What I did bring was passion, energy, and an actor's experience, the need to focus and memorize. He took a chance by hiring well outside of his norm and industry standards. After two months on the job, he asked me if there was anyone among my actor friends who might be interested in a job. Phil was more than pleasantly surprised by my relatability and the ease with which I could get people to listen, communicate, and invest. In a business that burned people out in months, I bounced from probation to junior broker in less than a month. I put in the time while applying my background alongside what I was learning. I came with no bad habits, which Phil suggested was probably a strong reason for my early and continued growing success. He also recognized that my ability to memorize meant I quickly learned the nomenclature of the business, market stats, and knew how to provide that information to others. I asked him once why he took the chance on me. He shrugged his shoulders and had told me some of the most qualified people on paper turned out to be huge disappointments. He also liked my enthusiasm, and he confessed he was curious as to how I would do in this environment, being that it was so structured. I told Phil that structure was no different from the expectations of a performer on the stage. You show up, you get your script, you do a table reading, and then you get off book as soon as possible while rehearsing, learning blocking, learning changes to that blocking, and then learning everything with new introduced elements such as props, set pieces, and technical. I explained to him that my job in the brokerage was no different than my role as an actor. As a broker, I was obligated to tell the truth while speaking to one individual. In theater, I was obligated to tell the truth to every single person in every single seat at the same time.

Regardless which side of the desk you are seated, your background, training and experience is part of your brand and who you are. When you hire a former theme park worker, especially one with any length of service under their belt, you are hiring a legacy performer and employee. They come capable of putting out a dozen fires at once while simultaneously communicating with several dozen people, remaining on script, and delivering the talking points they're expected to convey with precision. In most theme parks, new hires are taught that custodial is everyone's responsibility, and even if their role kept them in a backstage support position, they still learned the crucial tenets of excellent guest service. At Disney, Above and Beyond guest service is not only provided by the well-clad-in-plaid guest relations crew, it's the sort of experience one gets with many individual encounters throughout the course of a day.

Consider food and beverage workers in a theme park. If you find such a job listed on a résumé, ask the candidate if they spent time at a quick-serve dining location, character dining, or even a food and drink kiosk. Ask them if they worked at EPCOT during the Food and Wine Festival, Holidays Around the World, Festival of the Arts, or Flower and Garden Festival. If they worked in any of these environments, there is a strong likelihood that they saw more people in an hour than your operation will see all day, and that they handled the crowd with courtesy and efficiency, while safely managing their area. If you see Universal on a résumé, ask if this individual worked during Mardi Gras, conventions, or Halloween Horror Nights. Inquire if they pulled a double shift. Most of the time these are voluntary decisions, choices made willingly and happily by a theme park employee. They understand the need for staffing and can perceive when their park might be short on team members. They know what it's like to go on vacation and have to wait or deal with stressful crowds, so they do everything they can to be part of the solution. While you, as the hiring professional, have seen only one side as a guest, these individuals have seen both sides because they often visit the parks on their days off. Sometimes the visit happens on their own, and other times it's because they have family and friends in town who want the theme park experience. If you have friends or family who work at a theme park and you are reading this, there's a good chance you leveraged their connection and largesse. Next time you go to a theme park with someone who works there, pick their brain. You have an opportunity to peer behind the curtain.

A TYPICAL CAST MEMBER AND TEAM MEMBER'S QUALIFICATIONS/BACKGROUND.

It's important to remember, first of all, that a typical career track in either one of these companies is atypical when compared to just about any other industry.

Disney and Universal do a more thorough job of researching the individual applying for a position than just about any other company (it is a safe bet to say the US military and alphabet agencies likely do a more thorough investigative job with new hires, but that is to be expected). Why? Why be so cautious? Companies like Disney and Universal have a name and brand to protect. The culture of these two companies, while magical in many respects, may not be the right fit for everyone. Better to identify that during the interview process (at Disney, known as Casting). When it comes to Disney or Universal, few other companies stand up to the thoroughness by which they confirm someone is new-hire material.

Here's something else to consider when hiring a former theme park employee. Even if they don't initially know how to tackle a new responsibility, they always know where to start. You'll never hear a cast member or team member say, "I don't know." At Disney and Universal, people are trained to go into problem solving with a "yes, and" attitude. You also won't hear a former Disney employee dismiss something as, "Not my job." The reason behind this is simple. When you are hired into a Disney operation, the training entails expectations of partnership. You may work in a big wheelhouse, but you will never be expected to do something that falls under another department unwillingly. For example, if you work in an attractions operation and you have a problem with one of your doors or there's a loose handrail, you are not expected to grab a screwdriver and get to work. You reach out to a manager, or you reach out to maintenance, and they come to address the issue. Both Disney and Universal's park and resort operations are big on partnership. Cast members work alongside each other in an operation, but they will also join forces with other lines of business when the need arises, and it arises often. Assessing those needs and taking initiative to pull someone in is part of the day's expectations. Universal is no different. Think about the logistical partnership necessary to launch any one of their special events, or bring together people from different departments for a Habitat for Humanity housebuilding day. Partnerships, everywhere, get the job done.

It's not only the job that's important, but the training that's associated with the role. Training doesn't stop at onboarding. Every assigned park or resort has additional training themed appropriately to the park (as two examples, the second day of training at EPCOT is called "Discovery Day", and that of Disney's Hollywood Studios is appropriately called "On with the Show"). On the Job training (OTJ) directly at one's work location continues for the duration of employment. When new protocols or procedures are being rolled out, employees are trained up on these new procedures. As mentioned earlier, every single new hire at Disney and Universal goes through very specific and specialized orientation. Even if you are being hired into a backstage support role where you never typically interact with park guests, it is important enough for you to understand the culture and your part in that story, that the training is exactly the same as if you are being hired to a popular attraction operation.

When it comes to training and performance expectations, if everybody is not on board, things fall apart. Many of us have been to restaurants and stores where, because the training protocols were changed, the employees cared less or simply became apathetic. There's a certain big box do-it-yourself chain that prided itself on hiring individuals who came with the background of the department they would go to work in. That person in plumbing had experience as a plumber. The person in electrical? Same thing. Over time, they just started hiring people. The first time I walked into one of the stores and went back to the electrical department only to be told "I don't really know," when I asked a question? It was kind of a cultural shock for me. Most people don't know that if you have a question regarding medicine and its efficacy, whether you're talking about over the counter or prescription, a wonderful resource is the pharmacist behind the counter. Imagine asking a question about medicine for a cold and watching the pharmacist shrug their shoulders and say, "I don't know." In theme parks, if you're looking for a bathroom, or a place to get a bite to eat, you can approach any team member or cast member and there's a powerful likelihood they'll give you several options. As cast members and team members, when we go through the training, we are never told "I don't know" is not an option. Instead, we are simply trained to learn and know, and - when we do not know - to partner.

A Disney employee's résumé and background is unlike other backgrounds any hiring operation will encounter, especially for applicants coming from parks, resorts, and the Disney Cruise Line. Their job descriptions will be more than a couple of sentences, and frequently interspersed with different dates and details. The same holds true for Universal. One of my fellow stunt performers started out in attractions, at Jaws. He went from Jaws to do two stunt shows, became a stilt walker and trainer, and a safety rigger and performer for Halloween Horror Nights (HHN). When those shows ran their course (because things at theme parks always change and evolve), he moved on to become part of the park safety team. He continues to advise for HHN. I would frequently find theme park employees self-deploying across many different lines of operations. Prior experience with multiple departments gave them a foundation of applicable knowledge to draw from.

For example, the lighting director at one of my shows was frequently lending a hand to the maintenance teams for nearby attractions. His previous position had been in the maintenance department (he wanted to work for this company even though his background was stage production lighting). He had been at this location for years and was familiar with the rides. Instead of passing it off as someone else's job, he was always happy to go over and help when problems arose. He laughed that he could have had a second job and income as a park trainer. He was on the clock and didn't care (eventually he worked with the Documentation team to create a series of one-sheet reference documents for new hires).

I can count at least twenty-one roles and assignments I had within the Disney company during my two plus decades with the Orlando resort. They ran the spectrum of asset management to training. At any given time, I could expect to give a guided tour on the sound stages or manage a multi-million-dollar technical operation. My responsibilities and roles in live entertainment included everything from performer to stage manager, and oftentimes, there was overlap. With every new hat I wore, I was always mindful of the importance of excellent guest service. Whether they were day guests visiting a park, proprietors and managers with their computers, competitors in the Warrior Games, C-suite execs and Imagineers auditing and evaluating tour content, or cast members showing up for their day, I always saw these people as *my* guests. At Universal, even though my job title read "Performer", I was involved in everything from parade talent management to training. I count among these experiences special events, conventions and conferences, attraction grand openings, ad-hoc focus groups, program launches, and plenty of Mardi Gras Parades. For both companies, the reason why I performed so ably is simple: they gave me the foundation for action and response in orientation. We learned very quickly how important it was to preserve the character and integrity at the park through our actions. Everyone is also taught that opportunity exists everywhere. All one has to do is hope on the horse, grab the reins, and go.

There are plenty of people who have built a career out of working in a theme park, in just about every discipline possible. You will find them in attractions, food and beverage, technical maintenance, administration, and entertainment. In fact, for the latter group, many of these people who leave wind up being called back and contracted to do in-house training, voiceover work, or other audio work.

No matter where a cast member is, what they do, or what their title is, everything starts with leading a service-oriented operation. Where many companies must explain this to new hires, in theme park resort hospitality, every single employee understands the importance of being proactive. Even third-party vendors who provide a product or service at Disney Springs go through the same training as full-fledged theme park employees. Everyone with a Disney name tag is on the same page regarding the expectations of the company. Everyone is expected to do what they do, carrying out their tasks, mindful that excellent customer service is the not-so-secret sauce, the special and primary ingredient for a successful day on the job.

Don't believe it? Take a look at what you do to in service to your company or point blank, to generate revenue. Whether you own your own business, partner with someone else, have an online business, work for a small family company, restaurant chain, or a global conglomerate, it all starts and ends with service. The product, commodity, or widget you provide is secondary. If you think this is not the case, try taking even basic customer service out of the equation and see how long you stay in business.

Think about going to a five-star restaurant or resort. You go in with expectations beyond comfortable sheets, exquisite food, and beautiful views. How you are greeted the moment you arrive says everything. Those first few seconds set the tempo for the rest of your trip. Both Universal and Disney handle this in many ways. Staying at one of their resorts? How are you greeted when you pull up to the security host or hostess? At Disney, you are typically with a smile and a, "Welcome home." When you show up to one of the parks, there are people on the other side of the touch points with a greeting and a smile. They are eagle-eyed, and the moment they see you struggling (perhaps your ticket won't scan), they step in to intervene. Spend more than a few moments looking around, or staring at a map, and a cast member will more than likely ask if they can help you find anything. I always looked forward to engaging guests in this way. I could help them plan out their trip while getting to know where they were from and what they were looking for. All of that in a one-to-two-minute encounter.

As Universal visitors, we often approached a team member to ask about a ride, show, or food option and wound-up walking away with a new friend. On one trip, we asked the team member working at Hogwarts to confirm the trivia we heard about the attraction building actually housing props from the film. She told us she could do more than that and gave us an impromptu tour, pointing out dozens of things that never would have caught our eye were we left to our own devices. The *Harry Potter* fans among the group were buzzing for the remainder of the day. That is truly awesome magic. At Disney, I always encouraged cast members, whether they were new or picking up shifts in other areas, to locate the nearest bathrooms, the closest food stop, and learn the park hours. Everybody wants to know where the bathrooms are (speaking of which, here's a quick helpful tip for EPCOT: in World Showcase, bathrooms are located between countries, every other country. And they're air-conditioned, important to know with the Central Florida summers. You're welcome).

Excellent guest service includes all the typical courtesies, even between cast members. Third-party vendor services that might never be seen by a day guest, like backstage dining locations, bring the same energy as front-facing locations. Working cast and team members get to know the people serving food, making sandwiches, and running cash registers the same way a Disney Vacation Club member gets to know the concierge greeter who welcomed them at check-in. Courtesy is a piece of the puzzle that provides a working foundation for the guest. Even the security hosts and hostesses at Disney and Universal engage while performing their roles. They check your items, your bags, your strollers and frequently, your smiles.

Above and Beyond guest service is a non-negotiable for both Universal and Disney. It is repeatedly stressed throughout orientation (through examples and role play) and is something people are constantly evaluated on. Every single former park employee understands the importance of being there to make sure the guest experience is exceptional.

In any operation, a former theme park employee is an empowered employee, ready to take initiative and handle new problems as they arise. Everyone likes being recognized for their hard work, and at Disney, this recognition serves as encouragement to bring that same energy and team spirit every single day. Milestone work anniversaries are a cause for celebration both locally and property wide. Disney and Universal do so many things wonderfully well, and throwing parties is one of them. Go Big or Go Home is a secret marching order for them. I have never been to a cast celebration or Universal team member party that didn't result in jaw-dropping presentations and a wow factor to the nth exponent. It's the kind of recognition that helps people do their best work, because it confirms they are on track. Every one of us needs that recognition for different reasons. For theme parks who create such programs, they are carried out with exceptional enthusiasm.

As a result, even the most baseline employees in a theme park are empowered to take action in ways that teach and instruct. People take it upon themselves to make a difference. During my first tour of Disney, as an attractions host, I was still earning my Ears when I had an opportunity to spring into action. A young girl was walking with her father and not really paying attention to where she was going. She accidentally walked right into her dad and dropped her popcorn. Needless to say, she was devastated. I could tell from his facial expression that her father was processing what to do next (dad brain is indeed a thing). At that point, I approached the family and knelt down to speak to the girl.

"Hey, I saw what happened," I said with a smile. "I get distracted walking around here all the time. What do you say we get you a brand new popcorn. Would that be okay?"

She nodded and I stood up. "Provided it's okay with dad, of course." Her father also nodded and I walked them to a popcorn location. I explained the situation to the food and beverage cast member behind the counter, and she had a replacement popcorn in the young girl's hands before anyone could say thank you, and in less time than it took me to describe the scene.

No managers needed to get involved, no forms needed to be filled out. No trip to guest relations. At

Disney, it's up to the employees and their judgement calls to resolve these situations. They learn, and they are empowered to do so during their very first day as a new hire. Another great example of this happened on my first manager assignment at Disney's Hollywood Studios. I was doing a park walk with Uma, a cast member who would go on to become an incredible leader, the kind of guy everyone could get behind. His personality is jovial and fun-loving, yet he knows when to be serious. This guy believes not only in what he does, but the opportunities that it presents to everyone he interacts with. It is his character. I think no matter where he winds up in the company (and I am convinced he will one day be a VP), he will still have that serve-first, leaning forward mentality.

One day, during this park walk, I was helping a family get their bearings towards a restaurant where they had a lunch reservation. As I finished up with them, Uma came up to me. "Hey boss. I have a British family over there. I got them some towels because their little boy just got sick all over himself. I want to get him a new shirt."

I acknowledged it was a good call and walked with him to the closest merchandise location. Speaking to the cast member behind the counter, I let her know I'd reach out to her manager so that we (my line of business operation) could pay for the shirt. The entire exchange took less than two minutes and we had the new shirt in-hand. The family we were helping were beside themselves with relief. They took the shirt, and we went on with our day. For Uma, and many others who wear the Disney name tag, such examples are not the exception, but the rule.

At Universal, team members are similarly empowered. Whether it is an impromptu tour a piece of technology not working, they haver the discretionary ability to make things right, or enhance an already-wonderful experience. One night, during a parade, we were were on one of the ride vehicles at Universal Studios. As we came around the corner to disembark, the team member looked from me to the wide, grinning expression on my daughter's face, and asked if she wanted to ride again. You bet she did. He left us on the vehicle, and off we went. These sort of things happen because magic, courtesy, and the ability to make a difference in small ways is never discounted, and always encouraged. Hourly theme park employees are the conduit for most of the incredible moments that take place.

Managers and leaders of theme park operations do considerably more than their title might suggest. They are responsible for staffing, morale, and the daily budget. They have to manage VIPs. Sometimes there is a tour for executives from a sister park. Often times, they're doing all of this at the same time. Depending on the operation, they may be responsible for equipment or the attraction itself. A food and beverage manager is managing the restaurant, staffing, training updates, and liaising with the kitchen to make sure there is enough inventory to manage the expected guest flow. They must manage a budget beyond the present day, into the next week or the month. They will be tracking labor hours, equipment shortages, and key performance indicators based on guest feedback.

A park ops manager may be responsible for a specific attraction or an entire region. Their responsibilities may include ride vehicles, camera equipment, infrastructure, entertainment, food and beverage, or some combination of these things. Their daily operation includes ride or show testing, prop inspection and replacement (liaising with the right departments through all of this), staffing, training coordination, onboarding, and other things as they pop up. They do all of this while making time to sit through staff meetings, conduct one-on-ones, and do park or resort walks. Managers will spend a considerable amount of time out in the operation on a given day, and in doing so, they will clock a massive number of miles. I stopped wearing a tracker on my wrist to measure my steps the day I did more than a half-marathon worth of walking on the job…during a single shift.

You can never know what is happening in your operation if you are not an active part of it. If you spend your time backstage or in your office, huddled over a computer, you're going to miss 100% of the opportunities to make a difference and impress upon your team how important presence is. Managers who rely on their employees to provide a full spectrum of feedback on how the operation is performing are only getting part of the picture. Senior leaders who exclusively rely on managers to pass along concerns are being shielded from what they need to know. I've always admired the Proprietors, GMs, and VPs who made park walks and venue visits a part of their everyday schedule. They know what's happening because they see it first-hand, and they get an honest snapshot of their operation.

When I interviewed for a resort manager position at the Vero Beach Disney Vacation Club resort, I was told the expectation was to be on stage and in guest view 70 to 80% of the time. I told them I could do better than that because I already spent 90% of the time in the parks when I was working. It was not an issue for me because these expectations had been put in place for all of us, and because of that, follow-through was easy. To this day, a great core memory I have is of a park walk at Epcot with a fellow leader, John. We had so much fun walking through the park and stopping to talk to guests that by the time we had circumnavigated the entire footprint of World Showcase, we had spent almost six hours out among guests without a break. We were aligned in our personal expectations of how to perform in our operation.

This goes hand-in-hand with establishing expectations for your team. Without clear expectations in place, you're going to wallow in the dark trying to find your way. The major theme park entertainment giants excel at giving leaders the tools to establish expectations and build upon them. When a team knows the direction in which they should be moving, everybody arrives together. Managers will also conduct frequent pulse checks for their employees. It's not rare for managers to be aware of challenges and victories happening at a personal level. This is an important component to doing things the Disney and Universal way. When an hourly employee knows they can count on their manager, they are willing to do what needs to be done. This applies everywhere. The really good managers will go through quite a few pairs of good shoes and computer keystrokes, all the while making certain their people and their operation are in a good place. When your hourly employees know you are willing to go to bat for them, when they know you have their back, they will go above and beyond for the operation. That's something every single hiring professional should consider when they see theme park experience on a résumé.

SO…YOUR OPERATION IS HIRING.

Let's pause here to unpack Disney's orientation and onboarding process. It is important to recognize how robust it is when compared to hiring and onboarding as a process in the entertainment theme park industry and beyond. Disney orientation is removed from the way most of the corporate world functions. The focus of Traditions is to talk, teach, and learn about the history, heritage, and legacy of the Walt Disney company. It's preparing new cast members and crew members to be the next generation of storytellers. It is a figurative and literal handing over of the keys to the kingdom. The entire day is a give-and-take, one part entertainment and one part Socratic method. It encompasses a full day of training and learning. During that day, one quickly discovers the importance of teamwork and the pride and joy that comes from being a Disney cast member.

So, what exactly does the magic of first-day theme park orientation look like? Disney's Traditions is a day filled with multimedia presentations, interactive activities, and a park adventure - a huge deal if you've never stepped foot inside any of the Disney parks. The magic in fact starts when you first arrive at the Disney University campus. The facilitation team is there to greet you, answer your questions, and welcome you with a smile. While I was a Traditions facilitator, I always made it a point when we arrived backstage at the Magic Kingdom to ask my group who among them had never been to the Magic Kingdom before. One day will always stand out. An older gentleman in the back, Jerry, raised his hand. He had never been to the resort at all, let alone Magic Kingdom. I asked him to come to the front and told him he was going to lead us onto the stage. As he opened the gate to let us in, I waited to let everybody pass. Once inside, with the gate closed, I kept my eyes on him. Is a certain vicarious feeling that comes from being with someone who is experiencing something for the first time. It is one reason why we like to share with others the things that bring us joy.

He made his way to the center of what could best be described as a micro cul-de-sac, an area we cast members refer to as Center Street, and he stood there for a full minute before slowly turning in a circle and taking everything in. The sights and the sounds (in addition to the cacophony of day guests, there was an open window advertising voice lessons. You could hear the piano playing and someone singing along to the notes) told their own story. By the time Jerry was facing me again, and I could see his face, his eyes were welling with tears. I walked up to him and smiled.

"It's pretty magical, isn't it?"

He nodded. "You know," he started, "I moved to Florida to be closer to my grandkids."

"I've heard that a time or two," I said with a smile.

He continued. "I'm a retired cop from New York. I had a foot beat in the Bronx. Twenty years."

"Let me guess. With your background, you got hired into security?"

Jerry nodded, looking at the flower cart as if noticing it for the first time.

"There are a couple of components to your background that makes you so valuable in your new role. One is your obvious training and experience, but the second, and less obvious, is that as a beat cop, you spent a lot of time talking to people one-on-one."

He nodded. "If you make a difference in one person's life…"

I grinned wide. "My wife is an educator, and I've heard her say that repeatedly. I believe that I must do everything I can to make a difference. It's important. People always remember how you make them feel." I paused for a moment and then smiled again. "It's not the Bronx, but we're glad to have you here, Jerry."

He laughed. "No, it's not the Bronx, and that's ok."

Traditions is an intentional, amazing first day.

That experience happens more times than one can count, and not just in Traditions. The number of cast members I got to know during my two plus decades? Each one has enriched my life for the better.

I shared this story with Michelle, a former fellow performer and current executive at a Fortune 500 company. Michelle told me her experience teaching Universal's orientation program was almost identical.

She shared how program leaders for both parks exchange ideas on everything from training protocols to topics. She even went so far as to suggest, with the exception of the IP branding, it was possible to swap the two, and the experience for new employees would be virtually the same. Michelle shared how, when she was first hired as an entry level manager, she brought the Universal onboarding process to her new company. While her company's new-hire training is a pared down version, she confided the orientation process has had an incredibly positive effect on long term retention and morale.

I have a friend who I met when we both taught Traditions. She went from being an attractions hostess to being an attractions manager. There were tremendous opportunities for advancement at Disney for her, but she wanted something else. She really wanted to move and had a very special fondness for Saint Augustine, Florida. I completely understood that, because as a lover of history and culture, it gives and gives. She wound up taking an hourly position as a tour guide at a historical complex, close to the center of historic Saint Augustine. She told me when they saw Disney on her résumé, they didn't hesitate to hire her. She quickly advanced, and when she became an assistant manager, she introduced her version of an onboarding program which bore many striking similarities to those of Disney and Universal. The company she was with quickly responded by allowing her to create a training program. Along the way, she became the media and content manager. She told me one of the many advantages the new program delivers is retention of employees. The point here is you

have no idea what kind of superstar is living in the heart
of the former theme park employee whose résumé you
may be reviewing.

Let's imagine you're hiring. You see a résumé that
reads Disney or Universal (or even both). Let it grab
your attention. Take the time to talk with this person.
Even if they've only worked one role over the course of
several years, dig deeper. In almost every single case,
this prospective employee has dealt with guests on a
daily basis. If they worked in a setting facing day guests,
then the number of customers they saw was in the
thousands, every day. They may have been part of a
training program as a cross-trained employee, taking on
responsibilities in addition to the role for which they
were hired. If they are passionate about teaching, they
may have been part of the crown jewel of training
programs, Traditions. Like the initial hiring process for
Disney, landing a role as a Traditions facilitator isn't as
simple as just showing up and saying, "I'm here - put me
to work." At Universal, a live show performer could also
have conducted improv classes designed to help people
manage a variety of situations (these exercises are often
based on outlandishly sounding - but real - experiences).
The former cast or team member you are considering as
a new hire probably worked quite a few special events.
Things like limited pop-up events, conventions,
weddings, and after-hour ticketed events like Disney,
Sea World, or Universal's respective Halloween
offerings.

"Mentor" was never an official title on any on-boarding document I received, yet I did it frequently. Whether it was talking about the history and heritage of Walt Disney or asking questions to help flesh out someone's true direction, I found myself frequently in a position to provide additional insight.

One day, after one of our stunt shows, a cast member walked up to me and introduced himself. He told me he was a college program cast member and was leaving in about a month to head back to school. He wanted to know if he could talk to me and hopefully get an idea of what getting into professional entertainment took. He was interested in the tech side of things, and when I asked him why he didn't want to talk to a tech, he shrugged and said someone told him he should talk to me. For better or worse, my reputation preceded me.

We arranged to meet at one of the resorts after my shift. Over coffee, I learned he was truly passionate about performing, but he didn't think his parents would support such a desire. I asked him what *he* wanted. Without hesitation he said he wanted to perform.

"The only thing worse than not doing what you want is the regret of not even pursuing it in the first place," I told him. "If your parents love you, they will support you, even if it doesn't seem so at the beginning. If you know what it is you want to do, you will become an incredible force. They will have to get behind you. Parents want their kids to do well and be well. They are rooting for you." He told me he was going back to school and would consider everything we spoke about.

I heard from him about nine months later. He changed his major to theater and could not have been happier. The next time I heard from him, he had just completed a national tour of *Hello Dolly*, where he met his fiancé. He said they were still trying to decide whether they were going to move to Chicago or New York, but no matter what, it sounded like he had landed squarely in his wheelhouse. I can't and won't take credit for any of this. I simply made myself available to have a conversation with a young man who had some questions.

When you are hiring a former Disney or Universal employee for your operation, that person is more than an employee. They understand efficiencies, and they work through a model of Keys. Every new cast member learns about the Five Keys in Traditions: Safety, Courtesy, Show, Efficiency, and Diversity. No key is less important than the others, but Safety is the key that unlocks all the others. Diversity is important in both personal and business in ways you might not consider. Consider a simple hand gesture. For Americans, the "OK" gesture means something else depending on where in the world you come from. Being aware of and sensitive to diversified interpretation is the key between success and failure in an endeavor.

One theme park employee in your ranks is a half-dozen people you could hire out of any other industry, neatly packaged into one person. They might have showed up at Disney's Casting doorstep as unskilled labor (as many hourlies do), but they left with a full toolbox. In the arena of hospitality, former Disney cast members and Universal team members are the *crème de la crème*. They are empowered in their operation, whether custodial, food and beverage, entertainment, security, or park operations, to not just follow protocols, but constantly identify better ways of doing things.

This is not to say every single individual who gets hired is looking to push the needle. Some come to work for Disney, Sea World, Six Flags or Universal because it has always been their dream. People also come to find work at a theme park the same way they do anywhere else, because they need a paycheck. Many times, people go for the theme park job because they experienced the magic as a guest, and they want to preserve the magic for others. When you get that mindset in your company, incredible things transpire. Many people who come to Disney just because they need a job quickly discover that it's no ordinary job, but one where they get as much out of as they invest into it.

Theme park employees discover new ways of empowering their operation and improving it. The "Friendly Pantry" is a great example of this. I saw one of these first at Disney Photo Imaging. When I arrived at the operation, I learned that the coordinators, along with a couple of photographers, came up with the idea to create a stockpile of food and snacks. A large, two-door metal cabinet was re-appropriated for this purpose. If you forgot your lunch, ran low on snacks, had to extend a shift, or didn't have any money on you, you could help yourself to any of the Friendly Pantry's offerings. The only condition was that you had to contribute, and the preferred way was through replacement food of any kind. I contributed things like boxes of granola bars and, after a trip to a big box store, a unit of thirty individual Ramen noodle cups. It was a community effort and I'm pretty sure that if I happened to swing by in the next five minutes, I would still find that cabinet bulging with food.

During the pandemic, a cast member in Guest Relations went to work for a supermarket chain. There, she introduced the "Friendly Pantry" idea by creating the same food storage cache found at many a Disney break area. She didn't make a big deal out of it; she simply identified an area where she could improve and got to work. In return, the general manager of the store created a new role for her and asked her to document the process so it could be duplicated at other stores. She brought her Disney experience to the table several times, applying it everywhere she saw fit. So highly regarded were her contributions that, when Disney called her back, her general manager asked if she would consider picking shifts at the store whenever she could. He didn't care. He would take any time she was willing to share. That is an indelible imprint for sure.

Both Universal and Disney are entertainment companies, but they are also massive, global business operations. Every new hire quickly learns this. Both orientation and on the job training all emphasize why the three legs of business are so important. Employees for both companies learn the importance of meeting guidelines for personal grooming, performance, and expectations of the operation which include timeliness and other metrics. They understand why the leaning-forward attitude of putting others first is a key component. There are clear expectations regarding attendance, attitude, and accountability.

While some of the responsibilities and requirements of theme park work are perfectly similar to those that take place in your own operation, theme park employees always bring a vast array of experience that will enhance your organization. The glue holding all of this together is relationship-building.

Both Disney and Universal are all about relationships - they understand that a successful business is one where a leader takes care of employees, employees take care of the customers, and the customers support the business. Relationships are at the heart of what makes this process viable and successful. The former Disney employee you hire is showing up with a whole lot more than pixie dust. They are showing up to the interview with experience working under a variety of physical and meteorological conditions. They show up for work, ready to do what it takes, and they do this because they understand that relationships make a difference. Everybody works together even if they don't realize it. Teamwork makes the dream work. If you don't think relationships matter in your company, you are not paying attention.

The relationships that cast and team members build also extend to the guests. Plentiful examples abound of families booking stays at resorts, or visiting specific parks, attractions, or restaurants because of specific individuals who work there. Disney hasn't cornered the market on this, but there's a massive percentage of people who will plan a trip knowing the person who checks them in at Disney's Animal Kingdom Lodge will be there and has been there for the past seven years. They will go to a restaurant on a certain day or for a certain meal because one of their favorite servers is there. Shows, restaurants, and hotels all matter not because of the facility, but the people who bring those spaces to life. Theme park employees and guests will frequently exchange social media information and stay in touch. It happened to me many times.

That kind of magic doesn't happen everywhere. In fact, most hospitality engagements are transactional in nature. But if you want people to keep coming back, you must make it mean more. I remember it happening for me at Club Med's Sandpiper Bay in Port St. Lucie. I realized their leaning-forward attitude was exactly the same as Disney's. They encouraged their GO's (the abbreviated term for Club Med Employees) to get to know the guests, to dine with them and to share their own stories. One friend I made and have stayed in constant touch with, Curt, is a Krav Maga practitioner and circus performer. He knew about my stunt background, and I started teaching him stunts. Rarely do we contact each other and not remind the other of how fond we are of the relationship we have created. Another GO, who worked in one of the merchandise locations, invited me to her wedding. That sort of relationship building is pure magic.

Guests I engaged with in the park became friends and are still so to this day. This might be unusual in other business settings, but it tends to be quite the norm at Disney and Universal. This happened to me at the Six Flags park I worked at in the Netherlands, too. I have been invited to weddings, parties, and family get togethers because of these relationships. To this day, and no doubt for the rest of my life, I can say with tremendous confidence that most of my friends will be current and former cast members and team members. That's the sense of community working in a theme park forges between its members.

So if relationships are the beating heart of a viable business, then ask yourself this: doesn't it make sense to hire someone who has lived out the importance of forging relationships every single day? Their time working at a theme park is time spent growing and developing. At both Universal and Disney, your foot soldiers, the team members and cast members on the front lines, greet guests, know their managers, know their proprietors, and probably know the GM and VP for their area as well. They know people in other operations. They have friends in different lines of business. They know some of the guests who visit. For Universal and Disney (and even the Six Flags park I worked at), they are places where lifetime relationships are forged. Things are just things. People? That's where success begins.

Most businesses are siloed, and there's not a tremendous amount of communication between their individual entities. Think about a golf club. The people who work in the pro shop may know the folks running the golf course. They may be part of it. Or they may not. They may know the restaurant if they have access to the food, but if it's a "members only" club, they may not know anyone there except in passing. They may or may not know the grounds crew and landscaping crew who take care of the property itself. If there's a hotel attached, they may or may not know anyone at the front desk, in housekeeping, or in concierge. They may or may not know the management company. They may or may not know the people who reserve their tee times. They might not know their own managers. They might not even golf!

Even with the siloed nature of theme park operations, this is not the case at the parks and resorts. At Disney and Universal, there is a tremendous amount of cross-pollination and cross-utilization. In Disney's case, they maintain a platform called the Extra Hours Hotline (EHH). Here, a cast member can pick up extra shifts if they want, often in locations other than the one where they typically work. It's a great opportunity to learn about or get an in with a different line of business. Cast members can go to this platform and see what's available and then select a shift that piques their interest. In some cases (such as food handling), they have to meet certain training requirements or certifications before picking up additional shifts. In others, there is no additional training requirement. Food and beverage cast members will look for additional opportunities beyond their food service locations. Maybe they want to pick up a few hours doing crowd control or work an after-hours event. Sometimes it's simply a desire for a change of pace or scenery. If you spend your days indoors, on a food, prep line or taking orders, time outside in a greeter or parade position is a welcome change. These are great opportunities to experience and learn above and beyond the role they were hired into. It's a wonderful opportunity not only to see what else is out there, but to also meet fellow cast members and managers. It's relationship building and bridge building in the best sense possible.

Cross utilization (Cross-U) opportunities give people a chance to learn about a different line of business by being a part of that line of business. They range from temporary assignments to as-needed Cross-U opportunities. After Traditions inspired me to become a leader by title, my own managers supported me by helping me find these opportunities. They set up chances to shadow managers, and scheduled meet-and-greets for me, giving me the chance to spend a day alongside managers in attractions operations, food and beverage, resorts, recreation, and Disney photo imaging.

In a sense, I was a fish leaping from fishbowl to fishbowl. Everywhere I went, new managers and cast members were appraising me and my abilities. Unbeknownst to me, they were taking my pulse as a personality and trying to figure out how I might contribute to their culture. Within DPI alone, my experience went well beyond shadowing the photographers in the parks, there for our day guests. I also took part photographing at special events and resort offerings, such as "Chip and Dale's Campfire Sing-Along". I went to the ESPN Sports Complex and met the incredible GameDay photographers there. There was RunDisney photography support for the marathoners and Disney Entertainment Group photographers for weddings. As you can see, one role, that of photographer, came with more than a half-dozen possibilities. Other aspects of theme park work are just as varied.

Consider the diversity of opportunities that fall under one role. The person you're interviewing, or whose résumé you're looking over, who lists Disney Photo Imaging in their experience, is modestly excluding all the things that come along with the role. They don't mention the week they spent learning how to handle a $7000 rig with high-end technology. Or how taking photos of a first-time visitor to the Magic Kingdom is entirely different from snapping a picture of a Disney Vacation Club Member who shows up once or twice a month, which in turn is wholly different from photographing a bachelorette party or marriage proposal. These are different from coaching your family to get the perfect magic shot. On the résumé there is not the slightest mention of how they show up in all sorts of weather, for all sorts of shifts, during all sorts of holidays. Disney cast members learn, during their first day on the job, that, "We work while others play." That same message is burned into a team member's work ethic as well. There can be times of the year where a team member or cast member will see more of their colleagues and work operation than their families and home. They know what they are signing up for during the interview process, and that level of commitment is cemented during orientation.

Take the time to ask former theme park employees questions you might not otherwise. The person across from you might only be one physical body, but that body has worn multiple hats and done many different things. Sure, they may have worked in costuming. They were responsible for knowing not only where the costumes are in the inventory, but the peripherals, like hats, suspenders, and belts. They track inventory, damages, pieces that are lost, found, and they know the specialty items. They do more than that. They also pick up shifts in parades, food and beverage, VIP, and special events. Each one of these requires them to interact with a completely different caliber of guest. They've had access to leading edge technology and understand the importance of working under all sorts of conditions. Most importantly, they develop the ability to respond in the moment to a variety of different situations.

Bringing a former Disney or Universal employee into your operation means getting an individual who, even with the entry level amount of training, has already had thousands of dollars invested into them. Disney is not afraid of hiring and training people to be the best, and then watching them leave for the next opportunity, whether that takes them to another part of the company or beyond the gates of the Walt Disney Company itself. For Universal, the same mentorship and training mentality applies. The casting machine for both the Universal and Disney parks is slow and deliberate by design. The initial interview, additional screenings, background checks, and the probationary periods are designed to evaluate the individual even after being hired. Almost all theme parks have a probation period, but Disney and Universal do not make it a central element to their onboarding. These entertainment organizations always seek to make sure the time, energy, and money they are investing into a new hire is going to pay off. The hiring process is intended to make sure the right people are brought on board for the right positions, because they are acutely aware of the resources they will spend on each individual member of their team.

Remember, when you hire a former Disney cast member, it is possible you are getting someone who has already received more training than your operation provides. You're also getting someone who is a team player. They know that a combined effort achieves more. They are sympathetic, empathetic, and good at listening. They tend to be ideal problem solvers and are always looking for more efficient ways to do things. They don't do this because they are lazy but because they recognize that such efforts reward everyone. When you hire a former Universal team member, you get someone who has been empowered to make a difference. You get someone who understands the responsibilities and the standard operating procedures for a given venue, whether it is an attraction, a stage show, or a restaurant. These are individuals practiced in the art of continuously delivering a stellar guest experience without tarnishing the brand name.

Theme park employees possess above-average social skills, a plus when integrating into a new operation, working with new people, or interacting with your consumer base. Both Universal and Disney foster these behaviors and encourage their applicability no matter the position or location. Any time I spent up at guest relations at any of these parks, and including Six Flags, I witnessed in many of these employees a constant diffusing of challenging issues along with service recovery, while maintaining a calm and service minded exterior. Not every theme, park or entertainment, destination establishes the training background to create the service protocols, another reason why knowing the questions to ask, can help you determine if a candidate is a good fit for the operation in which you are hiring.

Over three thousand job classifications. That is The Walt Disney Company. Parks and resort operations make up a large part of that list. But remember there is also DVC, DCL, AbD (Disney Vacation Club, Disney Cruise Line, and Adventures by Disney), and Disney on Broadway. There's a very good chance the former theme park employee you are considering already has the skills that you look for in a new hire. Don't be surprised if, during the interview process, you find them asking you questions or presenting scenarios to you even as you pitch situations to them. Disney people are good at identifying how to plug-in. The vast majority of former theme park employees you see on your interview schedule show up with positive attitudes, multiple layers of customer service training, and a highly developed sense of teamwork. They understand such components constantly raise the bar in the workplace.

Simon Sinek does a great two-and-a-half-minute piece on performance versus trust. Anyone you hire out of Disney or Universal will be a dynamic performer you can count on. Remember, just being hired by one of these entertainment companies is an accomplishment; only one in ten gets the job. When it comes to vetting, Universal and Disney do much of the heavy lifting for you. This is an important consideration for these companies. That is why every individual goes through a thorough background check. There are additional in-depth background checks, depending on the role and responsibility. For example, if they are being hired as a driver, going into resort recreation, or fireworks, these companies apply conforming standards according to local, state, and federal laws. They do not take shortcuts or decide such requirements do not apply simply because it is theme park work.

Consider this as you look at the person seated across from you, whether physically or through a computer screen. Engage them. Ask them to talk about the standards by which their former employer measured performance. Neither Disney nor Universal deploy heavy-handed people to measure KPIs. That's what their onboarding is designed to do. Every sparkling new team member, cast member, and crew member learns the importance of engagement and servant leadership on day one. performance measurements are analyzed, make no mistake, but these are done proactively to make sure the very best product is made available to the end-user.

Once you've done your due diligence, you will find your new hire is the best investment you can make for your forward-looking operation. Regardless what your business is, you are in the business of service. There's a story behind how to achieve excellent service. Your story may be different from others. The possibility is overwhelming that this individual will be your next generation of torchbearer, storyteller, and leader.

ADDITIONAL INSIGHTS

Just as people come to work in a theme park or destination resort for many different reasons, they leave for a variety of reasons as well. However, the vast majority of former Disney employees will agree with the much-repeated sentiment, "Once a cast member, always a cast member." I also know plenty of former Universal team members who still feel they have a personal interest in the success of the brand. Many of the people who come from theme park and resort backgrounds frequently have wonderful, smile-evoking stories to tell. They speak fondly of their time, frequently relating a particular experience as if it was something that happened just last week. Over time, they tend to look past the challenges and issues of operations and individuals, speaking only in positive tones about the experience. That is a thing that separates those of us who come from a theme park background from those who come from nearly any other sort of work. Yes, these entertainment companies are corporate behemoths, but there's something else at work here. Relationships.

Where working in any other industry or business may allow you to develop relationships internal to the company, working in a theme park or resort operation is all about building relationships. Those relationships become friendships and more.

Walt Disney said, "You can design and create and build the most wonderful place in the world. But it takes people to make the dream a reality." His direction for his team and everyone involved was pretty clear from the beginning. In building Disneyland, he wanted to create a place where the entire family could spend time together, in a clean and safe environment. He empowered each and every individual cast member to look for opportunities to create magic and build those relationships, something that is still a key component which sets Disney apart, decades later. The empowerment to build those relationships, and the results? You cannot put a price tag on that.

Carl Laemmle opened his Universal City ranch to guests because he knew people had an interest in moviemaking. They paid a small fee for admission and a little more for a box lunch and the opportunity to walk around the two-hundred-thirty-acre complex. If there were active productions, these guest had the chance to talk to the actors and crew. Decades later, Universal would introduce a tram tour as a more efficient way of transporting guest to various locations backstage. It also allowed for the demonstration of various special effects in a safe manner. To demonstrate how various elements in a scene worked, team members picked audience volunteers to play roles. Sounds familiar because every theme park and Renaissance festival you have ever been to has done and continues to do the exact same thing. Getting audience members involved breaks the fourth wall of theater. It also invites every single member to be a part of the gag, the joke, or the show itself. When an audience member is brought onto a stage, or made part of the set or action, you are telling everyone else seated,

"Look. This person is one of you and you are now part of this."

Team members and cast members wear name tags with their name and either their hometown or favorite character on them. This is an icebreaker that makes the employee approachable and encourages an immediate connection. Guests to the theme parks wear celebration pins so they can be recognized and approached. This is also a come-talk-to-me icebreaker. This kind of symbiotic relationship-building is basic yet pays handsome dividends for everyone involved. Connecting is the first point of courtesy and this one element alone, shared in an interview, demonstrates the deep level of insight you have for relationship building in business.

With Universal and Disney, whether you are a CEO, HR specialist, or someone on the front lines, you'll readily recognize the importance of people who work in tandem towards a singular objective. When any operation is on point, it enriches its own employees, who enrich the people that come through the front gate, gangway or front door. Those guests, customers and patrons support and drive the business. Business 101, the three-legged stool of business. The company takes care of its people. Its people take care of the customer. The customers take care of the operation through patronage, consumption, and promotion.

What is Disney? It is so much more than the largest, single on-site, location-based employer in Florida. Disney land use, environmental planning, and urban development are three elements that were considered extensively during the building of Disneyland. For every park and resort thereafter, these elements are foundational keystones. Equally as impressive is the fact these aspects are featured in urban planning courses and certifications found in colleges and universities throughout U.S. coursework. College-level classes to grad-level projects incorporate Disney-developed applications of city planning, crowd control, and traffic management. Disney is committed to continuing education, both at Disney University and through their college program. Disney has a charitable division, where they give enormously to the local community.

What is Universal? Like Disney, it is a first class, global entertainment giant for which the sun never sets. It is a company that has defined certain aspects of entertainment such as audience participation and bold entertainment choices so cutting edge, other companies are lining up to replicate the results. In some cases, they are the indisputable leaders for certain holiday events. Universal introduced Halloween Horror Nights, a special ticketed event that has endured for decades and has theme parks all over the world striving to create their own versions. Their production teams work with students from film schools, giving them the opportunity to shoot on location at Universal Studios, creating content with high production appeal. Universal also offers tuition reimbursement, volunteer outreach, and a host of internal-only opportunities designed to celebrate their employees and remind them of the valuable part they play.

At the heart of both of these companies is a deeply understood belief that growth happens only because of the people, but people are only part of the growth. The other part is community engagement. Both Universal and Disney offer masterclasses on what successful partnerships look like. Both organizations recognize the importance of deferring to experts in a certain class so they can continue excelling in their own lane. Some third-party vendors and business partnerships for both companies span multiple decades. Before the phrase "masterclass" entered the lexicon of constant (and some might argue exhausted) usability, Disney and Universal quietly employed it, one park, one experience, one resort, one patent, and one person at a time. Even their individual onboarding orientation programs stand out for how engagement can and does elevate the hiring experience.

A new hire, no matter what line of business they enter, could do much worse, but not much better, when it comes to the opportunities for growth, development, and career maturity. Where some companies might proudly boast how an executive started in the mail room or as a waiter in a restaurant, both of these companies can list example after example of various individuals who started in food and beverage, attractions, resorts, operations, entertainment and administration - people who, overtime, became managers, leaders of leaders, GMs, VPs, and more. In these environments, such opportunities to grow and develop exist because both companies make those opportunities readily available for those who see the value in both the culture and the chance to grow with the company. Both entertainment organizations also see the value in those who simply want to be part of their respective magic and not be obligated to climb a promotional ladder. There truly is room and a place at the table for every single individual.

Disney and Universal build such loyalty in part because of how they treat their employees. Such people become loyal because they believe in the cause, they appreciate the environment, they are thankful for the way they are treated, or all three. For many, being a part of that next generation of storyteller really drives home the adage that sometimes it is truly better to give than receive.

Give people a reason to leave and they will. Give them a reason to stick around and you will have created an environment that fosters growth and creativity. If you create opportunities to have fun, to grow, to career track, or just to simply have a decent job one can be proud of, people will not only stay, but others will seek to replicate whatever secret sauce is behind such forward-moving development. Every company has the choice on whether they want people to stay or go. The really good ones recognize they are building leaders who may just leave to lead another organization. When someone leaves your operation because of the excellent training, development, and career mentorship you provided, you should celebrate; this is not a bad thing. You have launched an ambassador of your brand and your culture who will always reflect positively on the environment they came from.

The best sort of interviews are the ones where happy accidents of discovery are made. These often happen because the recruiter takes the time to get to know the individual. When you are in an interview, no matter what side of the table you're on, you get to ask questions and learn about each other. That is enriching and empowering. Asking questions is both the Disney and Universal way in training, support, and customer service.

When you work for either company, you are placed in the unique position of being able to chart your own future and blaze your own path. Edutainment, the marriage of education and entertainment, is there for everyone, young and old, be they a guest, team member, or cast member. When we learn about the world in general, we learn about ourselves. When you are paying attention, both companies through their processes and opportunities teach you to reach for and become the best version of yourself.

Working in a theme park or resort operation means you carry the experience and training with you well after you have surrendered your ID. You develop filters and benchmarks for excellent guest service. It's incontrovertible that you will apply those measurements everywhere you go..

I will caution you to remember this one thing. If you have the urge in a new position at a new company to say, "Well, at Disney, we do it this way," or "You know, at Universal, this is the process we follow," don't. Grab that trusty notebook and make notes. After ninety days, sit down with your leader and share those insights but only as they are directly relevant. The danger of marching around a new operation, telling people how you did it in a theme park setting (or your last job in general), is more likely to get them upset and resentful of your presence than delighted you're pointing out the failures and shortcomings as you see them.

You do mean well. I know it. You know it. But it's always best to wait and learn how things are done before you decide to undo those things.

When you work for a place like Disney or Universal, you make relationships that will last the rest of your life. My closest friends are current and former cast members and team members. Many of them are relationships that not only endure, but strengthen over time. Those are relationships forged both when I have been a guest, and when I have been an employee. The intensity of those relationships spans long term friendships to enduring couple-hood (i.e. marriage). I cannot count the number of marriages between cast members who met at Disney. I met my wife at Disney. I have friends who met as team members at Universal and married. Maybe the potential for wedded bliss to happen in any job exists. It's possible to forge that union over the creation and presentation of a sandwich, smoothie or slide deck. In a theme park, however, the environment of sharing, of working together, of creating dynamic experiences, seems to have no small part in forging these unions. Besides, how wonderful must a person be if they like the same shows, attractions, theme parks, or holiday celebrations as yourself? It's easy to check off those boxes when you do it with a partner.

A theme park job is not just a job; it is also a job. It is an experience that constantly taps us on the shoulder, asking us to look at ourselves and the world in general with kinder, gentler eyes. For everyone who enters the theme park, whether showing up to work or to experience, it is reassurance. It is nostalgia. It is visual and heartfelt comfort. That applies just as much for cast members and team members because a considerable number of them were once guests in the park, long before their name tag. For everyone, the wide-eyed excitement of guests as they visit for the first time is a constant refilling of that magical pixie dust bucket. That thrill is just as palpable when we are enjoying a park or resort alongside a friend or family member, seeing and feeling the newness vicariously.

The experience provides for us the optics of an anything-is-possible perspective. Working in one of these operations, no matter what you are doing, is frequently a pinch-me experience. So many people I have spoken to left "serious" careers with onerous expectations because they'd had enough. If you are pouring sixty and eighty hours into work weeks to put your family in a better place, yet you never get time to spend with your family, what is the point? It reminded me of a comment Lee, my neighbor, made to me during a conversation. We talked about the tax of long hours on one's person and family. He nodded and said, "No one gets to the end of their life and says, 'I wish I would have worked more'."

They don't care that they might be starting with less pay, a wide spectrum of hours, and the fact they would be working year-round in Florida weather. It is nostalgia, or a family reunion, or the very first time they went to one of those parks. Those small, almost imperceptible moments took root until the little sprig became a towering oak. For that, these theme park new hires walk away from law firms, Universities, the aviation industry, Fortune 500 companies, and everything in between.

"I have to be a part of this, whatever this is," is something I have heard more than a time or two.

Consider the custodian I had a conversation with. It was the end of the night at Disney's Hollywood Studios, and guests were still trickling out of the park. I watched as he took his small broom and dipped it into his dustpan which held water instead of debris. He then proceeded to draw Goofy's face right there on the corner, where the sidewalk met the street. When he was done, he had more than two dozen people around him, mesmerized. They applauded him. Many took photos of the artwork and some kids even took pictures with the custodial cast member. He saw me watching, and there was no way I could conceal the smile on my face. Why would I, anyway? As I approached, I told him I thought it was nice work. He said, "I love what I do." I nodded and told him I understood. We talked for a bit. He told me he'd been with the company for all of six months and just wanted to get a job in the park. He said it had always been a dream of his. Where had I heard that before?

This young man happened to work in custodial, but it by no means defined what he did. I made sure to get his name, which was Cameron, because I wanted to give him a Keys recognition card, which is an internal way of recognizing above and beyond performance. I knew the company would be okay, and the guests would be well cared for, with people like Cameron there to make a difference. He's exactly the next generation of storyteller Walt anticipated walking through the Casting door.

Theme parks become a filter, and a modular plug-in application for many things life-related. As a constant, for people both guest and employee alike, the theme park experience is transformative. It is also, as mentioned previously, reassuring. Look at Universal. Even if they do not have the luxury of real estate in which to perpetually expand, as the Walt Disney World resort does, they maintain the bungalows and Central Park, two examples of spaces designed to reassure by remaining constant and familiar. Reassurance is not just about an old, familiar attraction or building. It's the other sights and smells. It's the attitude of the individuals wearing the name tags. It's those helpful smiles and nods. It's a sense that everyone you encounter is part of something bigger, and that something wants to include you. And don't for a moment discount the familiar face of a cast member or team member you have grown to share significant parts of your own life journey with. Meeting people who met at the park as guests and then became a couple is wonderful. When they come back the next time to show off an engagement ring or baby bump, that is amazing. But when they come again, to introduce the new addition to their family, that becomes next-level all together.

Part of that reassurance is also faith and belief. These companies and their park properties are going to remain steadfastly present. Disney is not going anywhere. Even if that ride you enjoyed as a child is no longer at the park, nostalgia combined with new experiences brings those memories right back to the forefront. With my two plus decades, I was afforded the opportunity to enjoy the nexus of being in a work environment where my family could always visit. That could have been the stunt show, it could have been character dining, or even the dinner shows. I spent many years doing this and always appreciated the fact I got to be a part of the magic-making in action. But it was illuminated for me in ways I could never have imagined. Whether it was the dancing and Polynesian cuisine at the "Spirit of Aloha Dinner Show", the music, food, and fun at the "Hoop Dee Doo Revue", or meeting Mickey, Jasmine, Aurora, Donald, or Tiana, I came to understand deeply and viscerally what *We Create Happiness* truly means.

For every individual who struck up a conversation with me and asked me if I enjoyed working in the parks, I would smile. I would tell them I am paid to be there and be a partner to the magic making. I get to make friends, I get to help people plan their holidays, I give them helpful hints and trivia if that is what they want. I will work with a team of individuals to ensure the surprise proposal goes off without a hitch. I would also tell them how cool it was that my family would reach out to me and suggest we all have dinner in Morocco after I was done with my day. How cool is that - that at the end of my day I get to go have dinner with my family in Morocco? As to the relationships I had built? I once took out a pontoon boat from the Contemporary resort to treat my family to a floating lunch on the water experience. Ready to pay, the cast member getting the boat set up told me she appreciated the Lights Motors Action tour I did for their area and wanted to reciprocate. Such opportunities and the relationships they create are not shabby at all.

Those opportunities don't just exist at theme parks. I recall a story of someone who worked for an international resort brand. They took it upon themselves to create a bunch of things that didn't exist, like a weekly newsletter with facts not just about the company but the industry in general. They took it upon themselves to create holiday celebrations and to decorate the break rooms. They convinced the general manager to order celebration pins for couples and families coming to stay who were celebrating everything from birthdays and graduations to weddings and anniversaries. Several things came out of this self driven initiative. The GM gave them a project day a month to work on magical moments both on stage and back stage. They were also given a weekend getaway for their family and one of the executive suites, and because of a partnership with a cruise line, were afforded the opportunity to take a trip with their family.

Even if you are not that motivated or driven, and that's OK, there's still plenty that you have to remember you are capable of. If you come out of a theme park environment, you know add an expert level things like crowd management, conflict resolution, and guest service recovery. Don't hesitate to remind the HR person during the interview of your capability to lead others and to defuse the situation.

It is important to remember brand loyalty takes a long time to build. Once it's established, whether you are an employee of a company or a consumer of what the company provides, you will continue to be loyal for as long as they continue to satisfy your expectations. Theme park, resort, and cruise line employees and their long-time guests all have the common trait of appreciating what the company is, what it represents, and how the organization treats others. Treat people well and everything else works out. This is a great objective to apply in life and business. No matter where you are and what side of the counter you are standing on, show people you care and they will reward you with the sort of loyalty and dedication money cannot buy.

Don't take care of people and you'll feel the repercussions.

I have helped enough individuals navigate the casting and hiring process and I've mentored enough people to know that working in a theme park or a resort associated with one of these companies is so much more than just showing up to a job. Work at one of these companies, especially in their theme park and resort divisions, is the exact opposite of a dead-end job. Those who left theme park and resort employment, many of whom I have spoken with, acknowledge endless opportunities in every direction. Even those who found the culture of a particular kingdom or company did not align with their own values or expectations still recognized pathways of growth, promotion and learning. Disney and Universal empower their employees. This sort of self managed I-can-fix-it mentality can often be found in higher end resorts. That sense of responsibility can sometimes be overwhelming. On the other hand, very few organizations promote from within and from the bottom up like entertainment and resort operations. If you're looking for an opportunity that comes with a heaping helping of adventure, work at a theme park or resort will tick the boxes as you get promoted because others see your value. With every operation you move to, you learn new things.

In what might be a surprising revelation to some, quite a few individuals I spoke with regarding their Disney careers told me the training and skill set they developed enabled them to leave the company, taking on a new role and set up responsibilities with another organization. One of my managers, a leader of leaders, left the company to become a Director of Entertainment for another entertainment organization. Another friend, who also had been with Disney, leveraged his media training when he left the company to take on the role of Media Director for a large sports franchise. Actors leave stage shows to do Broadway tours or perform on Broadway. Stunt performers go into film and TV and even become coordinators, filming and directing action sequences. Guest Relations tour guides become production coordinators for film companies. Plenty of examples abound of these opportunity leaps. Both Universal and Disney are good enough at what they do to constantly and consistently press out leaders who take the reins in other industries.

The opportunities when one leaves either of these companies are truly endless.

In your next role, gig, or job, if you find yourself thinking about whether or not something is *Good Show*, or you see active problem solving as a better way to address the customer experience, that's your theme park background and training at work. It is something just about any prospective new employer will appreciate. If you are in a serpentine queue waiting to check in at a resort, and you see nine or ten people spread out behind the counters but nobody doing anything because of an IT ISSUE, and you are wondering why they're not out there talking to guests about the delay and maybe engaging them both as a learning piece and a distraction, that is your theme park and resort background at work.

As a recruiter or hiring rep, when you onboard a former theme park employee, in most cases you get someone constantly evaluating the operation for opportunities to make the experience better for all those involved. Down the road, you may learn of company-wide rollouts for some of these practices. The former theme park employee is not surprised, because the mantra, "You spoke, we listened," is more than just words at Disney or Universal. They are action triggers in a place where ideas from the front line get traction all the time. The same thing that happens to high end branded resorts and destination resorts.

Just because cast members and team members learn how to make magic doesn't mean your operation is constantly going to be bombarded with it. That new employee who is a former theme park worker, manager, or executive is quite capable of having 100-proof truth conversations, too. They are more than capable of making observations and taking action. They are just as capable of observing and listening. Expectations dictate action. As a hiring rep or manager, making sure your expectations are clear on how the new hire can and cannot contribute when it comes to challenges within the operation will help all parties with their performance alignment. Action to get things done is just as important as the other A, accountability. As an hourly employee in a theme park operation, you understand the importance of self accountability. When you are leading a team, you understand the accountability applies not just to yourself but everyone who reports to you.

I've made this comparison before and it still stands. Hiring a former cast member or team member into your operation is analogous to a major airline hiring a former military pilot into their flight deck ranks. That new employee comes with a toolbox filled with tools ready to use, some of which may not even exist in your line of business. They not only show up with the skill set of commanding the aircraft, but they also come with built-in regimens of standards and protocols. They show up understanding that even though there may be just one, two, or three of them in the cockpit, it takes a team to get the aircraft away from the terminal, off the ground, and safely to its destination and arrival gate.

For those who leave the comforting space of wish-granting and magic-making, don't be sad because it's over. Celebrate the fact *you* were enlisted to be a purveyor of that magic-making. So many more people than you have wanted the chance to be in that position. You were given that chance and granted that power, the power to make dreams come true. I know plenty of cast members and team members who left Disney or Universal for a new opportunity. At their new operation, they accomplished a great deal in a short period of time.

Sometimes the old guard at a new company, those individuals who have been with an organization for a very long time, finds such hyper-drive engagement challenging. Some people simply bristle at change. But for many others, a smarter or better way of doing things is often greeted enthusiastically. You, with your theme park background, come with the experience and the mindset that in the theme park environment, one ever present constant *is* change.

One person I spoke with shared that she brought her scheduling and organizational skills to an operation that desperately needed it. In her theme park world, Kellie built Standard Operating Guidelines (SOGs) for various departments. She created monthly checklists designed to provide wellness checks not only for the operation but the people who made the operation work every single day. She single-handedly created a culture where people no longer felt like vessels alone at sea, but instead felt and performed like well-coordinated flotillas. About a year in, a Leader of Leaders at Disney reached out and asked if she wanted to come back. She had a conversation about what her return looked like. She then spoke to the owners of the company, a husband-and-wife team. Kellie shared something interesting with me. She said the husband seemed a bit sad - disappointed wasn't the right word, she told me - but the wife's reaction surprised her. When she was done explaining what the opportunity at Disney looked like, both owners smiled. The woman told her she had done more in a year to optimize their operation than they had been able to do in ten years.

"Girl? You got this!" she said to Kellie. When they worked out the terms of transitioning back to Disney, she agreed to check in once every three months with the owners, to advise and make any adjustments as needed. Just one more example of the power of a Disney background.

During an internal reorganization of in-park operations, one of my former leaders who had become a friend found his position being eliminated. We hear about this all the time in the corporate world. Such actions are frequently necessary if a company is to survive a current challenge or crisis. Other times, it's because the position no longer serves a need, or is found to be redundant. When I learned of this reorg, I went to talk to him about it. A part of me felt I needed to be there to comfort him in what might've been a time of loss. I knew him well enough to know that most of his adult career had been spent with this company. I felt very connected to him, and we shared an excellent rapport. I asked him if he was sad or angry or frustrated or upset. His answer surprised me.

"Ron? I love what I do, and I love what I get to do. Now? I get to talk about what I did. The fact is this: just because I am no longer employed here doesn't mean I won't still be an ambassador for the brand. I love the parks and the product as much as I always have. I love the people who make it happen every day. I love the people who save up so they can come and stay in one of our resorts and visit our parks once a year. I love that I got to know interesting people like you. I just don't have to get up at four in the morning anymore to make sure the pixie dust bucket is polished for the employees and the day's guests." He had the biggest smile on his face as he told me this, and it was clear his love for the company and the brand itself was unwavering.

Even in reorganization, the company still took care of him. He received a severance package which he wasn't expecting. He also received his Silver Maingate, so he, his wife and family could visit the heart of where magic happens - the people - whenever he wanted. He reminded me of the thing I always reminded College Program cast members. Disney was not going anywhere. Whether he was coming back as a guest, or decided to come back as a cast member, Disney would be waiting.

A friend from Universal had left Universal, did a tour, went to Disney, left Disney to go back to Universal, and ultimately left the theme park industry, this time for good. I asked him why he was convinced this time was the time. He told me he had a talk with his wife and they both wanted to launch a production company. He'd been in conversations with a few key players in the Atlanta area and it all made sense to both of them. He told me something I completely understood. He shared that the knowledge and experience he gained with both Universal and Disney more than prepared him to build this company with his wife. He was not sad. Quite the contrary, he was pretty excited about their future prospects, and the fact he had enjoyed so much time working at both Disney and Universal. I know a few couples who work together, who cannot imagine not being around the other, and it's truly incredible to behold. For these two, it was exactly the same.

If encounters with the people we are meant to meet during our journey through life make us better people, my journey with Universal, Disney, and Six Flags made me the best person I have ever been. My years at these places gave me friends who are more like family, people who are still in my life today. The wonderful souls among them count themselves among my tribe. I know if the right theme park or resort opportunity appears on my radar, it's an opportunity always worth considering. For anyone with a theme park background, anyone whose experience was magic, "never say never" is stenciled into the back of their brain. For every single individual, whether they ever go back or not, the mindset will be: once a cast member or team member, always a cast member or team member.

I know and made peace with the fact (although it was difficult at first) that it is okay to step aside and let others make magic in these environments. Whether I ever go back or not, it does not change the fact I had the experience, an experience I have become all the better for. I am not the only person that feels that way. If your time with a theme park or similar destination came to a close, and you moved on to your next opportunity, there's a very strong possibility you feel that way, too. One thing is certain. The very first time I walked up Main Street, and I saw those cast members smiling and waving with their Mickey Mouse hands, I knew I had to be a part of that. It was the people then, just as it has always been the people throughout my time at all of these parks. When I talk with those who had a less-than-magical experience, it is always tied back to an individual who might have been a colleague or manager in a location. Exploring that a little further, it turned out only a small part of that experience was less than magical, but so many other things more than made up for it. Those things were not the costumes, or the sometimes-crazy holiday hours. For all of us, regardless which side of the turnstile, table, desk, or stage we are, the thing that makes the difference? The people. For many, the bad experiences over time are easily brushed away, while the good times, with great people, are fully embraced. They are the core memories, the stories worth retelling.

It will always be the people who make the experience. That is life both inside and outside of the theme park world.

As Walt Disney himself said, "It's just been a sort of dress rehearsal, and we're just getting started." Sometimes that first run at a theme park or resort was a dress rehearsal of sorts. You can leave the operation and the company, convinced of its finality, only to find yourself submitting a résumé or CV at the prompt or behest of a friend or employee. You might be on tour, you might have landed at a fortune 500 company, you might be teaching at the University of your dreams. Yet some thing is missing, and that feeling is just visceral enough to cause you to schedule that interview. Like the tumblers in a lock, you find another perfect fit and discover that maybe, just maybe, never say never does not apply. In the situations which are more common than we realize, "no" actually means "not now."

Your life is simultaneously a dress rehearsal and two minutes to places. It is also showtime. We are constantly learning, growing, and applying. Until you are ready to step on stage and out of your comfort zone, keep honing your skills and keep your eyes on every opportunity that appears, whether directly in front of you or on your horizon.

The first step always starts with you. Whether it is the next question you ask, answer, or the next role you seek, keep building yourself as you build your tribe of supporters and proponents. Call upon your skill set and put yourself out there. Great things await.

You are just getting started.

BIOGRAPHY

Ron is a mostly retired stuntman with decades of experience two-wheeling cars, jumping off of things, being shot off of things, and clowning on both sides of the camera, all in the name of art. He is also an audiobook narrator, a writer, a podcast host, and a contributor for articles on business development, leadership, and content creation of all kinds.

He collectively has over four decades of experience in theme park entertainment operations, and several decades in film, TV, theatre, and live show venues.

At Disney, he held quite a few hourly positions. It was when he became part of the 40th anniversary Traditions team that he found his calling and knew he wanted to lead. The logic behind that decision was simple: if he could reach so many individuals as an hourly position, he knew he could impact more as a salaried leader.

Ron has created teaching and training content for Disney University, conferences and conventions such as IAAPA and InfoComm, and various stages. He served as a subject matter expert for Disney Institute and has given several talks on Disney Leadership. He has also lead forum discussions on Servant Leadership, a leaning-forward, people-first mindset made popular by Robert Greenleaf. Among some of the operations and venues at The Walt Disney World Resort Ron has supported or served are: The Polynesian Resort ("The Spirit of Aloha Dinner Show"), Fort Wilderness ("Hoop

Dee Doo Revue"), EPCOT, The Magic Kingdom, Disney's Animal Kingdom, Hurricane Ride-Out teams, Disney's Hollywood Studios, and the ESPN Sports Complex. His time is not limited to the Walt Disney World resort in Orlando. Ron's experience also includes almost two decades at Universal Studios Orlando as performer and trainer in a variety of roles, and several years with Six Flags, worked both at Six Flags Holland (Walibi), and the Six Flags Atlantis waterpark.

His appreciation for the friendships, relationships, and opportunities - thanks to the world of theme parks - cannot be overstated. They provided a tremendous foundation upon which growth continues. That foundation has been the basis for much of his success as a leader. He looks back on his days at the Walt Disney World resort, Universal, and Six Flags with tremendous fondness. They remain a collective experience like no other.

He is the author of <u>Oaken Rings</u>, <u>Lost in Adventureland</u>, and co-author of the Rocky Horror Picture Show narrative about life in a RHPS shadow cast, <u>Confessions of a Transylvanian</u>.

To learn more about Ron, his work & passions, and to contact him, visit his website: <u>www.ronfoxmedia.com</u>.

ACKNOWLEDGEMENTS

It takes a team to make anything move. Whether sports, a theme park, a motion picture, a cruise ship, or a book, there is no such thing as a self-made anything. What we accomplish happens through the partnership and guidance of those around us. As the saying goes, "If you want to go fast, go alone. If you want to go far, go as a team."

Thanks to:

E.M., Graphics. From concept to creation, all was enhanced was because of her. Such individuals elevate the quality of our lives in all forms. She tirelessly reminded me "good enough" never was, and encouraged me well beyond the point of exhaustion to exceed even what I believed to be my own limitations. She is a daily reminder of all that is possible in the world.

E.H., my Editor on this project. With an arrangement both engaging and thoughtful, Elizabeth puzzled sentences and sections into an order that made intuitive sense. She worked with purpose.

Mark. His detail-oriented, analytical eye made for a manuscript without distraction.

KT. Accountability partner. Kevin is as good as they come, when it comes to accountability partners.

So many shared with me their park, resort and cruise line experiences. Key among them was Gaia. With her experience on land and sea, both as a Disney College Program Cast Member and as a Crew Member, Gaia offered wonderful insights on the similarities and differences of both. She was also the first person to tell me it's OK to get out of the way and let others make pixie dust.

Brandon. The talks about Disney, theme parks in general, and the operational expertise similar to the military make for some great late night chats on comparison and contrast. Thank you for the endless insights.

Eric. He confirmed what I thought when he told me this was exactly the sort of book many people could use. He called it a "Life Learning Manual for Modern Times." I wouldn't go that far, but if every person who cracks the spine of this book gets one thing out of the text, that is a good thing.

A deep and meaningful thank you to every single cast member, crew member, and team member who shared their stories, experiences, ideas, and insights. To a person, they moved the story forward. I would need a separate chapter to thank each of them. Their contributions and insights were tremendously helpful to painting the picture here.

The acknowledgements section is an important section to writers because the key players mean the difference between something soaring or being stuck, the immoveable force, on the ground.

These key players are the details, and they include you, the reader. I hope you enjoyed the book and share it with others.

This collective effort embodies and epitomizes the expression:

Teamwork makes the Dream work.